PRAISE FOR *THE DISCIPLE MAKING CHURCH*

Highly recommended!
—*The Presbyterian Outlook* magazine

There is no person I know of more qualified to address the
greatest need in the church today—that of showing how the local
church can grow vital disciples— than Glenn McDonald.
—E. Stanley Ott
President, The Vital Churches Institute
Author, *Twelve Dynamic Shifts for Transforming Your Church*

This book has had a lasting impact on many readers.
It could have the same effect on you.
—*Dynamic Steward* magazine

Why should congregations shift from programmatic-driven
organizations to disciple-making environments?
What does such an environment look like?
McDonald answers those questions in clear, convincing language.
Lay leaders and congregants can profit greatly from his insights.
—Herb Miller
Founding editor of *Net Results* magazine
Advisor for the U.S. Congregational Life Survey

Revolutionary!
—The *AgapePress*

The book will have a lasting impact on you
and your walk with the Lord.
—*Christian Book Previews* magazine

Shows how biblical discipleship is possible
for today's Christians.
—*The Indianapolis Star*

McDonald definitely moves us in the right direction because
he is not concerned with constructing a list of things to do
during the week but that we become transformed people.
—*Equip* magazine

THE DISCIPLE MAKING CHURCH
FROM DRY BONES TO SPIRITUAL VITALITY

NEW REVISED AND EXPANDED EDITION

THE DISCIPLE MAKING CHURCH
FROM DRY BONES TO SPIRITUAL VITALITY

GLENN MCDONALD
foreword by E. Stanley Ott

FaithWalk
PUBLISHING

©2004, 2007 Glenn McDonald
Published by FaithWalk Publishing
5450 North Dixie Highway, Lima, Ohio 45807

Scripture quotations, unless otherwise indicated, are taken from the HOLY BIBLE, NEW INTERNATIONAL VERSION®. NIV®. Copyright ©1973, 1978, 1984 by International Bible Society. Used by permission of Zondervan. All rights reserved.

Scripture quotations marked KJV are taken from the Holy Bible, King James Version, Cambridge, 1769.

The Message by Eugene H. Peterson, copyright © 1993, 1994, 1995, 1996, 2000, 2001, 2002. Used by permission of NavPress Publishing Group. All rights reserved.

Printed in the United States of America

12 11 10   7 6 5 4 3

Library of Congress Cataloging-in-Publication Data

McDonald, Glenn
  The disciple making church: from dry bones to spiritual vitality / by Glenn McDonald.
      p. cm.
    ISBN 0-9724196-8-3 (alk. paper) (2004)
    ISBN 10: 1-932902-67-8; ISBN 13: 978-1-932902-67-9 (alk. paper) (2007)
  1. Church growth. 2. Church renewal. I. Title.
  BV652.25.M22 2004
  253-dc22
                        2003021398

DEDICATION

To the disciples of Zionsville Presbyterian Church,
whom I am privileged to call my flock.

ACKNOWLEDGMENTS

Everything I've learned about discipleship I've learned from other disciples. I am eternally grateful to God for sending the men and women who have relentlessly shaped my life.

Special thanks to Bob Jordan, my friend and partner in ministry, whose encouragement and laser focus on the disciple-making task are fresh every morning. Special thanks also to Dallas Willard, whom the Spirit has uniquely gifted to proclaim to this generation the Church's mission of being disciples who make disciples.

Mary Sue, Mark, Katy, Jeff, and Tyler graciously surrendered their husband and dad to the computer for the entirety of a beautiful Indiana summer, and loved me all the way through it.

Thanks to Dirk Wierenga, Louann Werksma, and Ginny McFadden of FaithWalk Publishing. It's a joy to be in partnership with joyful hearts.

CONTENTS

FOREWORD

When visiting a city where I lived years earlier, I worshipped with the congregation whose pastor had been a wonderful encouragement to me before his retirement. I was surprised to discover it difficult to find a parking place; the sanctuary was packed and the hallways and classrooms were jammed with people. The worship service was a pleasant experience and the current pastor was a sound preacher, but nothing was sufficiently gripping to explain the tremendous attendance I had witnessed. I happened to have a friend who was an elder in that church. I phoned him, inquiring about what had led to the immense vitality I had just witnessed. He explained that during the time the pastor I had known served that church, his major work was to give his people the heart, vision, and passion for growing the people in their lives as disciples of Jesus Christ—those in their homes and neighborhoods and places of employment. After he left that church, while new pastors and new programs came and went, the people went right on encouraging one another in Christian discipleship.

I was impressed. That congregation had become a disciple-making church in a way that matches Glenn McDonald's description of a disciple-making church. Such a church is one in which the people of God understand God's call on their lives to make disciples. It is a congregation where the people in dependence on the grace of God have the heart and the know-how to make the growing of true disciples a reality. For such a congregation, disciple making is clearly a lifestyle to be lived before it is a program to be run. It is a lifestyle centered on an unambiguously expressed set of defining practices, practices that result in the spiritual growth of followers of Jesus Christ.

In the last half of the Twentieth Century, congregations increasingly began to rely on programs as their primary means of growing disciples. We do know that activities, groups, and programs centered on disciple-making practices can, indeed, bear some fruit in the growth of disciples. However, what typically happened in many churches was that programs and activities became increasingly separated from the central issues of discipleship development. Such programs became a form of spiritual entertainment, enabling a group to listen passively to a speaker while asking little life change from the audience. We know that the most effective disciple-making occurs in the impact of "life on life," as my friend and mentor, Jim Tozer, loves to say. One life models, teaches, and encourages another life to love, to follow, and to grow in knowing the person of Jesus.

Glenn McDonald leads us to consider the impact of life on life, the impact of your life on the lives of the people around you, and how your personal relationships are the essential conduit through which you may encourage another person to grow in faith. McDonald teaches us to ask key questions such as, "Who is your Barnabas?" That is, who is the person encouraging your faith? "Who is your Timothy?" That is, who is the person you are encouraging in Christian faith? Such questions help us move from some general affirmation of disciple-making as a significant calling on every Christian, to the very specific practice of actually growing real people as disciples through real acts that result in the relational impact of life on life.

Words like "disciple" and "discipleship" are often bandied about without a clear explanation of what they mean. Suppose you want to develop the discipleship of those in your family or of people you know from your church, neighborhood, or place of employment. Do you have a clear idea of what that would practically mean in their lives? Making disciples means having a grasp of what discipleship is all about and being able to express meaningfully what the identity and activity of the follower of Jesus Christ really are. Being a disciple means that you are one who trusts in and follows Jesus Christ, growing in his likeness and committing your heart, mind, soul and strength to obey and serve him.

Once when I was thinking about such questions in my own ministry the image of a person popped into my mind with an arrow pointing away from the person. I thought of that arrow as an expression of everything that defines what a disciple is to be and do: in short, the description of a mature disciple. Finding a way to describe such a mature disciple summarizes the fruit we seek to grow in our own lives and in the lives of others in the process of disciple making. Glenn McDonald offers a marvelous expression of the profile of a disciple centered on six defining practices, the six marks of a disciple that, as he puts it, describe "what it means to be like and to live like the Son of God."

Glenn McDonald knows of what he writes. As the founding pastor of Zionsville Presbyterian Church, he has emphasized disciple making as an integral part of that vibrant congregation's DNA since its beginning. All of us long for our congregations to be vigorously growing disciples who are developing dear and deeper relationships with their Lord and who are God's instruments of that blessing in the lives of the people around them. McDonald gives us a clear pattern our congregations may follow to move by God's grace into the excitement of a truly disciple-making church, no matter what level of disciple making we currently experience.

E. Stanley Ott
President, the Vital Churches Institute

INTRODUCTION

ASKING THE RIGHT QUESTIONS

Early in the life of our congregation, at the close of one of our monthly board meetings, I posed my standard pread-journment question: "Are there any other concerns or new items of business that need to come before us?" I yawned and glanced at my watch. It was nearly 11:00 p.m. I was confident that everyone intuitively grasped the right answer to that question: "No, absolutely not."

One of our board members, however, had already raised her hand. "I'd like to know something," she said. "How long do you think it would take someone visiting our church to hear about their need for Jesus Christ, and then know how to act upon it?"

Silence filled the room. This was no ordinary question. It couldn't be addressed numerically. It couldn't be answered pro-grammatically. I knew that this question struck directly at the heart of what we all agreed was our reason for existence. And now, when push came to shove, none of us could answer it. We agreed to pon-der the matter, do whatever research we could, and then pursue a follow-up discussion the next month.

What did we conclude? Four weeks later we admitted to each other that, for all our apparent organizational success, *we had no comprehensive strategy to transform as many men, women, and children as possible into lifelong learners of Jesus Christ*. We had plans to keep growing, but no plan to grow disciples. We could present seminars burgeoning with helpful principles to effect change but could not articulate what any person in particular would need to do in order to become as spiritually healthy and vibrant as possible.

And I didn't have the faintest idea how to get started.

Disciples, Not Just Decisions

Please understand: If you had approached me at any time during the early days of our church I could have summoned a legion of words to describe our mission and would have footnoted every major point with Scripture. I wouldn't have *sounded* as if I were skipping along the surface of what God was trying to accomplish.

But words are cheap, especially theological ones. It's easy for church leaders to invest sixty hours a week in chores that bear the stamp of supreme importance—crafting a newsletter, directing a meeting, composing a presentation—while spending fewer than six minutes a week in reflecting on the overall mission of the church. Busyness masquerades as the business of heaven. To paraphrase Jesus' closing words in the Sermon on the Mount (Mt 7:21–23), "Not everyone who says to me, 'Lord, Lord,' will enter the kingdom of heaven, but only the one who does the will of my Father who is in heaven. Many will say to me on that day, 'Lord, Lord, did we not prophesy in your name, and in your name drive out demons and perform many miracles? [Didn't we establish the best youth ministry in town, assemble an awesome praise band, and wow everybody with our annual attendance figures?]' Then I will tell them plainly, 'I never knew you.'"

"*I never knew you.*" That's the rub. And that is our Lord's most solemn assurance that "doing church" is not about tactics and programs and prefab kits for conducting ministry. It's all about relationships.

For the better part of the last century, North American churches have tended to define success by the number of people who have made decisions. Who exactly has prayed the salvation prayer at the back of the little booklet? How many children came to our Vacation Bible School last summer? How many individuals have crossed our line of membership, or joined a small group, or participated in one of our mission trips?

To be sure, when Jesus said, "Follow me," he was calling for a decision. As churches, however, we have tended to excel at the theology of decision-making but have by and large failed to develop an appropriate curriculum for disciple-making. We have struggled to find ways to help ordinary people get beyond the choosing of particular Christian activities and to learn how to think, act, and be like Jesus in every possible respect, every day of the week.

Six Relationships and Six Marks

Today I am convinced that if our aim is to develop churches characterized by *disciples who make disciples*, we will make the most progress by asking the right questions about the right kinds of relationships. The first half of this book will explore six such relationships from the perspective of the apostle Paul:

Who is your Lord?
Who are you?
Who is your Barnabas?
Who is your Timothy?
Where is your Antioch?
Where is your Macedonia?

Whenever we surrender the quest for the Next Best Program as our standard way of doing church, and rely on the spiritual transformation that happens uniquely through relationships, we are committing ourselves to a path that will seem both mysterious and unpredictable. Nevertheless, there is something definite that characterizes every discipling relationship. There is a cherished set of learnings—a time-honored curriculum—that informs the task of being and making disciples. The second half of this book will detail what we have come to call the **six marks of a disciple**:

A Heart for Christ Alone
A Mind Transformed by the Word
Arms of Love
Knees for Prayer
A Voice to Speak the Good News
A Spirit of Servanthood and Stewardship

This is not a list of "six things I need to do this week." The six marks are the essential description of what it means to be like and to live like the Son of God. They represent God's continuing call for every person in every relationship. To quote the old saying, "getting people into heaven" is undeniably important, but it hardly exhausts the mission of the local church. If we're doing anything less than getting heaven into people—right here and right now—then we have misunderstood the force of Jesus' "Follow me."

For whom are these pages intended? If you are a leader of a Christian body that is in transition to a disciple-making focus; if you are part of a small group that is looking for a more holistic way of being together; if you want to ponder the ramifications of a life of fuller obedience to Christ; if you are seeking how to better frame the questions and issues for a strategic-planning process for your church; or if you simply want to know how God might bring greater spiritual vitality "to a dry and weary land," then by God's grace may these pages encourage you as you go forward.

One compelling question—uncomfortable and oddly timed as it was—helped our church to make a crucial turn. Asking the right questions and identifying the right relationships is still the need of the hour, because such reflection always precedes a journey in the right direction. Knowing what to leave behind at the start of such a journey is crucial. That's where we'll begin.

1

FAREWELL TO THE ABC CHURCH

My one-and-only personal experience of mountain biking came in the middle of a family outing to the Rocky Mountains. Not far from the place where we were staying, a ski lift was transporting warm weather visitors to the top of an Alpine ridge where, for a couple of bucks, anybody could rent a mountain bike and go zooming down the hill.

Our then eleven-year-old son Jeff and I were the only "takers" for this new experience. Together we hopped on the chairlift and began the 12-minute ascent to the top. We hadn't gone very far when Jeff turned to me and asked what turned out to be a crucial question: "Dad, when was the last time you rode a bike?" To be honest, I had no idea when I had last gotten on a bicycle. From my vantage point on the ski lift, however, I could see parents and kids of all ages biking down the mountain. How hard could this be?

The helpful young lady at the rental counter fitted me for a bike and a helmet. She then gave me a quick tour of the gears on my handlebars. I was floored to learn that there were twenty-one different speeds. "Dad," whispered Jeff, whose embarrassment about being seen with me in public was steadily growing, *"everybody knows that."* The rental agent concluded by emphasizing, "Here are your two hot gears, for those moments when you really want to pick up speed." *Great. We'll keep that in mind.* Off we went on our cycling odyssey.

I had already identified the bike trail that seemed custom-made for us. It was called "Cinch": four-and-a-half miles of twists and turns through towering pines and quaking aspens. I pedaled once, just to get started . . . and that was the last time I needed to pedal my bike for four-and-a-half miles. Gravity took hold of us and yanked us down the mountain.

Most of the way I was scared to death. I squeezed the brakes so tightly that my hands began to ache. In fact we stopped a few times on the trail just to give them a rest. I was so nervous about losing control and launching myself over some hundred-foot precipice— and hoping that at least they'd spell my first name with two *n*s on the memorial plaque—that I literally ended up hurting myself in my attempt to slow the pace.

Not everybody who rides mountain bikes has my kind of experience. Every now and then, as I squeezed the brakes harder to maintain control, we would hear other bikers coming up behind us. "Coming left!" they would shout, and before I even had time to react they were flying past us in a blur, then down around the next corner and gone. I couldn't believe it. Their bikes were identical to mine. What did they have that I didn't have? They had trust. They had learned that their bikes were perfectly capable of handling mountain trails at great speed. So was my bike. *I just never let go of the brakes.*

If the love of Jesus Christ has found a home within our hearts, then we are the carriers of an awesome power that is simply waiting to be unleashed. From all eternity God has chosen to grow his kingdom through us. And it's unstoppable. It is stronger than the force of gravity. How do we know this? Jesus said, "The kingdom of heaven is like a mustard seed, which a man took and planted in his field. Though it is the smallest of all your seeds, yet when it grows, it is the largest of garden plants and becomes a tree, so that the birds of the air come and perch in its branches" (Mt 13:31,32).

But somehow, instead of marveling at the ways that God's life is capable of exceeding all our limitations, we have managed to find the brakes. We're even willing to hurt ourselves—to hold ourselves back—instead of trusting that God wants to transform us into people who are just like Jesus of Nazareth, and to use our lips and our hands and our availability to produce other disciples.

Learning Our ABCs

I should know. In 1983 I was called to be the organizing pastor of a new congregation on the suburban fringe of Indianapolis. In my mind I cherished a sincere but poorly focused desire to "do church" a different way—to help generate new strategies for recruiting and releasing committed followers of Jesus. It didn't take me long, however, to find the brakes.

At the end of year four, by God's grace, a few dozen pioneers had grown into a flock of three hundred. Along the way, however, our attention had become increasingly riveted to the ABCs of congregational life—attendance, building, and cash. How many people are on site, and is that number increasing? Is there room for everyone to park, and when can we upgrade our nursery facilities? What was last month's bottom line, and will we have the money to pay next month's bills? Without even noticing it we were paying more attention to structure than vitality. Our lip service to "releasing God's transforming power" had become swamped by our let's-keep-the-place-under-our-control behaviors.

We instinctively began to keep score on the basis of externals—the institutional surface of the Body of Christ—and awarded ourselves high marks for our apparent health.

The ABC church is alive and well in the United States—if we can bring ourselves to use the words "alive" and "well." It's safe to say that a large majority of Protestant congregations have made attendance, building, and cash—as opposed to Christ's Great Commission in Matthew 28:18–20 to be and to make disciples—their organizational bottom line. Without question, effective institutional management honors God. Every gathering of Christians, large or small, has to manage an appropriate agenda of "business." But business is not why we are in business. Some of the fiercest blasts in Scripture are reserved for those who would hold back the rush of God's Spirit for the sake of polishing the organizational apple.

The Word That Transforms the Wilderness

As I pondered the ease with which we turned our attention to church management, I found myself captivated by Ezekiel, an Old Testament prophet who was handed one of the most depressing of job assignments. The bulk of his public ministry required him to be the bearer of bad news. He groaned, ranted, and even mimed a series of sermonic vignettes that declared the wide gulf between God and the people of Israel. After nearly three dozen chapters, however, the tone of Ezekiel's book suddenly softens. It's as if we've caught sight of the first crocus of spring poking its head above the snow. In 37:1–3, Ezekiel receives an unforgettable vision:

The hand of the Lord was upon me, and he brought me out by the Spirit of the Lord and set me in the middle of a valley; it was full of bones. He led me back and forth among them, and I saw a great many bones on the floor of the whole valley, bones that were very dry. He asked me, "Son of man, can these bones live?"

Confronted with a vast skeletal heap—the pathetic, unburied remains of who knows how many people—Ezekiel has no answer. He feels helpless. The situation appears hopeless. "O Sovereign Lord, you alone know," he sighs. It would take a miracle to bring life and hope to this valley of death. The prime business of God, however, is imparting life and hope.

Then he said to me, "Prophesy to these bones and say to them, 'Dry bones, hear the word of the Lord! This is what the Sovereign Lord says to these bones: I will make breath enter you, and you will come to life. I will attach tendons to you and make flesh come upon you and cover you with skin; I will put breath in you, and you will come to life. Then you will know that I am the Lord.'"

So I prophesied as I was commanded. And as I was prophesying, there was a noise, a rattling sound, and the bones came together, bone to bone. I looked, and tendons and flesh appeared on them and skin covered them, but there was no breath in them.
(Ez 37:4–7)

When God's word is spoken, reality is transformed. "And God said . . ." and there were photons and cumulonimbus clouds and wildebeests and slime molds and burr oaks. Dry bones are no match for the word of the Lord. It's worth noting that in Hebrew the word for "word" is *debar*. In English there are a variety of prefixes that negate the meaning of a word—"non," "in," and "un," for example. One Hebrew way of achieving negation is to affix the letter "m" to the beginning of a word. When "m" is added to *debar* the result is *midbar*—the Hebrew word for "wilderness." According to the biblical mindset a wilderness is a "wordless place"—any site where there has been no transforming word from the Lord, a place where all hope has dried up.

Bones, but No Breath

Tens of thousands of American congregations have the feel of spiritual midbars. There may be a cherished memory of the last time God's transforming word was heard—a past event or a joyful season or a distinguished pastorate—but a present sense of expectation that God is about to do something new has all but disappeared.

5

Numerous churches that were launched with a compelling future orientation are now looking backwards, hoping against hope that a past golden age might somehow be recreated.

In Ezekiel's valley of dry bones, God speaks about the future. What follows is the celebrated Stephen King-like scene of acres of dry bones clattering together. Tendons and flesh come next, and skeletons progressively morph into figures that give the impression of human life. But note Ezekiel's important observation: "But there was no breath in them." In this wilderness experience, form precedes life. Structure arrives before vitality.

Again, I can certainly relate. With all my heart I believe God spoke our congregation into existence. Almost overnight we became an ecclesiastical Big Top sheltering dozens of smaller organizations—circles, committees, and coffee klatches. Structures almost magically appeared. But the breath of God was a good deal harder to find. Our passion for making disciples was a sideshow effort at best. Because we had no vision larger than being a top-drawer ABC church, our benchmarks for success became the acceleration of attendance, success in the next building campaign, and financial black ink.

Aside from a preoccupation with management issues, the ABC church generally exhibits four other characteristics that nearly always prove to be disciple-making liabilities. The first is a tendency to look for programmatic solutions to problems, challenges, and opportunities. Is there a new package on the market in the area of stewardship? What techniques are working for reaching out to disenchanted members? Has anyone come up with a fresh curriculum for training deacons? How about a 3-day seminar that will be our booster shot for evangelism? The only less effective strategy than scrambling for a new ministry kit may be summarized by the letters RLYP: *Run Last Year's Program*.

Programs are poor substitutes for vision, and completely unacceptable as any Christian group's reason for existence. God's will cannot be discerned from a resource catalogue or downloaded from a one-size-fits-all package.

A second standard feature of the ABC church is the tendency to rely on hard work as the way to go forward. If the program isn't producing, we'll step up our efforts. If the goals aren't being realized, our leaders will simply have to keep a few more balls in the air. Classically, North American congregations have relied on a single individual to generate church-wide progress in bringing people to maturity in Christ. That person is the pastor.

For roughly 300 years, Protestant pastors have been charged with the spiritual development of everyone within the church's reach—a mission to be accomplished through preaching, teaching, worship leadership, counseling, direction of appropriate boards and committees, home visitation, correspondence, administration, janitorial duties, praying at civic functions, and whatever other "hats" might be required apparel at a particular church. The ultimate issue therefore becomes: How can we expose a maximum number of people to the work of our pastor, so that he or she can work a maximum amount of spiritual magic?

The Incredible Shrinking Heart

Early in the history of our congregation I succumbed to this grocery list of expectations. At root was a powerful element of pride. After all, wouldn't our church be impoverished by the absence of my remarkable gifts and insights, served up regularly seven days a week? Determined that I would never have to answer to the name "Reverend Slacker," I found myself pedaling my inner bicycle faster and faster just to stay even with the demands of a growing congregation.

The costs were high. As a young Christian I had been thrilled every time I had heard others share something of their personal spiritual journeys. My heart had practically jumped. Several years into the rigors of church planting, however, I felt more like the mythological figure Sisyphus, pushing the rock toward the top of the hill again and again, knowing that it would inevitably roll all the way back down to the bottom, initiating another Sunday-to-Sunday cycle of total effort. At that point, when I heard someone speak of a spiritual breakthrough, my heart monitor was flat-lined.

When at home I tortured myself by thinking, "I ought to be out making calls right now. What kind of pastor am I?" When out making calls I couldn't help but think, "I ought to be home right now. What kind of husband and father am I?" Guilt became a 24/7 traveling companion. I was exhausted. Drop-in guests became interruptions. I frequently wondered how I would get through the next week's obligations. Mostly I yearned to run away, or to live out my fantasy of sleeping for three days straight.

On the outside I faked my way through my required church relationships, saving my major letdowns for those at home. It occurred to me that I was metaphorically living out one of those black-and-white science fiction films from the 1950s, *The Incredible Shrinking Man*. In the movie a man is exposed to a cloud of radiation, whereupon he immediately becomes a smaller and smaller version of himself. Doctors and scientists are powerless to arrest his shrinking. Ultimately he takes up residence in his daughter's dollhouse. The most familiar and friendly aspects of his home become threatening. Finally he tumbles down the basement stairs, wages war with a common house spider, and . . . well, you can catch the ending yourself sometime late at night on cable.

What was happening to me? I was the man with the Incredible Shrinking Heart. My heart for God, for ministry, and for my wife Mary Sue and our four children was progressively getting smaller. The familiar surroundings of my own home actually became threatening, since walking through my own door reminded me that I wasn't being the person God had called me to be. "Can't you see how hard I'm trying?" I would snap.

In a perverse way I took heart from the fact that historically a number of Christian leaders have struggled with less-than-ideal marriages. I wondered if marital tension might be a necessary price to pay for doing work in the kingdom. John Wesley's wife allegedly once rode up on a horse behind his open-air audience and shouted, "Don't listen to this man! He's out of his mind!" About the time Mary Sue started taking horse-riding lessons I became more than a little worried. But what could I do? God was multiplying the attendance, building, and cash of our congregation. Surely it would be immoral to slow our momentum just because I couldn't keep up.

Two major Hollywood productions featuring volcanic eruptions were released within a few months of each other in the mid 1990s. The movies *Volcano* and *Dante's Peak* have some intriguing similarities. Both feature a rugged male lead, a renegade whose instincts outshine the combined wisdom of those around him. Both these heroes report to bosses who play things safe, reject their sage advice, and thereby end up putting people in harm's way. In each case the hero makes brilliant decisions on the run that deliver others from peril. Most intriguing of all, however, is the fact that as each movie opens, the lead actor/savior is on vacation. Naturally each man materializes at the office and assumes the mantle of leadership from admiring coworkers just in time to save the day.

Far too many church leaders are convinced that their absence from the front lines of ministry for any period longer than three days will automatically trigger a flow of lava. How can an indispensable person justify a vacation, anyway?

My domestic world finally imploded on a day that I was running off to lead a weekend retreat. I remember standing on our stairs, holding a pile of papers under my left arm. Mary Sue was standing at the top of the stairs over a pile of laundry. We were yelling at each other in frustration and rage. I was conscious of the fact that the children could hear us. We were yelling at each other because our worlds had grown so far apart. Emotionally we had taken our hearts off the table of our marriage. I knew I had to do something. I had to make a point. Assertively I took a step up the stairs and growled something like, "I just want to know one thing: What happened to the beautiful woman I married?" With calmness and coldness Mary Sue lowered her voice and said, in effect, "Oh, that woman. She died. But you were very busy at church and you didn't see it happen."

In anguish I walked to our front closet and ripped my jacket off its hanger—in the process dislodging and shattering a Christmas ornament that I had inherited from my grandparents. The most valued things in my life were breaking up. Who could ever put them back together?

A New Way Forward

God could. Over time God presented to Mary Sue and me the opportunity to heal our marriage. On the other side of some excellent counseling, the support of our small group, and a thousand small acts to put our hearts back on the table, we reclaimed the dream of being a couple who can know and experience the love of God together.

It took crises in my personal and public worlds to convince me that the call to make disciples is not a clergy-dependent exercise. First I had to reject the assumption—all too common in the mind of the program-oriented church leader—that if I should step back from my manic pace of life, the kingdom of God would be just one day away from collapse. A healthy rethinking of my approach to ministry also required a proposal to our board shortly after our church's fifth birthday.

"With your approval," I said, "I'd like to try something different. I'd like to stop attempting to touch every activity in this church. I'd like to challenge the idea that somehow I'm the only player on the team who can carry the ball. What if we gave some of our lay leaders the training they needed and turned them loose in their own areas of ministry?" They had never heard me say this before. How would they respond to a pastoral request to step back from ministry?

The board members nodded, smiled, and said, "Why don't we start immediately?" Frankly it was unnerving to discover that my noninvolvement was welcomed as such an asset. They were, in fact, right on target. The members of our congregation felt freer and more valued as they were entrusted, in my absence, to invest in ministries and relationships that mattered. Without realizing where we would end up, our church had taken a vital step toward achieving a disciple-making environment. We had agreed that it wasn't crucial for everything to cross my desk.

This brings us to the third counterproductive tendency of churches with ABC priorities: Far from being challenged and empowered to do great things for God, rank-and-file church members are chiefly expected to be compliant. In his book *The Fifth Discipline,* leadership guru Peter Senge describes the multiple levels of personal ownership that are on display in most organizations. Generally only a few members can be said to be fully committed— that is, wholeheartedly sold out to the vision and ideals of the key leaders. All others in the organization align themselves consciously or unconsciously along a descending scale of compliance. In the average church, for example, we are likely to encounter each of the following levels of "buy-in":

Joyful compliance. "I admire our church's leaders and I will gladly follow them, even if I don't always understand their decisions."

Formal compliance: "Since I'm a member here it's my duty to be a good soldier and do what the leaders expect."

Grudging compliance: "Do I really have to do this?"

Noncompliance: "I'll follow my own path on this issue, thank you."
Malicious compliance: "Sure, I'll do their stupid program— just to prove how wrong they are."
Apathy: "What's for lunch?"

(Currency Doubleday, 1990, pp. 219–220)

In a program-based congregation there is a hope (usually a futile one) that large numbers of individuals will magically choose to be fully committed to the mission of the church. More realistically, pastors of ABC churches settle for a situation in which a majority of church attenders consent to be at least formally compliant—that is, in exchange for less than passionate devotion to Christ they will not rock the organizational boat. What are the dual norms for such a culture? Uninspired leadership and spiritual mediocrity rule the day.

Pastors who picture themselves as solo shepherds tend to become wrapped up in addressing a set of questions about their own performance: How am I coming across? Am I keeping it all together? Does the flock appreciate my care? Such leaders are far less committed to helping ordinary people grow into spiritual champions. Discipling relationships are unfortunately seen as dependent on the pastor's touch. There is little or no vision that individual Christians ought to be learning discipling skills in such a way that they can pass the baton of imitating Jesus to someone else—apart from the pastor's active intervention. As long as church leaders are blind to the power of investing in self-replicating relationships among lay people, and limit their flocks' potential for spiritual growth according to their own calendars and biological frailties, those congregations will make little progress toward fulfilling the Great Commission.

Letting Go of the Brakes

A fourth characteristic of the ABC-oriented church is the overt or implied use of control. Only a few individuals are granted permission to do ministry. "No" is heard more often than "Yes." When it's time to make decisions, only a few opinions are considered valid. Trust is extended to a handful of people, but not to *just anyone*. That would be risky, chaotic, and...well...inappropriate.

What would happen if McDonald's ran its franchises like the average local church? A skillful but frazzled manager would be seen throughout the day taking orders, making change, salting the French fries, and assembling Big Macs—all while six other employees behind the counter stood off to one side, applauding politely and gushing, "I'm so impressed with the way you spread the special sauce. I could never do that. And the deft way you put those ketchup packets in the bag. You've had training. You've been to hamburger seminary."

McDonald's wisely made a different management decision and thereby pioneered a global food industry. Even though there are burger geniuses and market specialists within the corporation, they are rarely seen by the public. When you and I approach the counter we are most often met by teenagers earning a minimum wage. Early on, McDonald's chose to entrust its future to the success of recruiting, training, coaching, and releasing ordinary people to carry out its most essential task: serving customers in such a way that they will want to return to McDonald's next week. In contrast, few congregations have concluded that their own members are worthy of such trust or are equal to the task of being the prime transmitters of God's good news to the next generation.

ABC churches, in summary, are more preoccupied with structural issues than with spiritual vitality; tend to seek programmatic solutions to problems; rely on the gifts, energy, and overfunctioning of one or just a few key leaders; value an environment of command and control more than giving permission; and expect little more than compliance from church attenders instead of world-changing personal transformation. Such congregations are certainly capable of achieving stated goals. They can grow in numbers, provide and maintain an appropriate facility, and meet financial obligations.

The dirty secret of the ABC church, however, is that its goals are far below the bar that is set in Scripture. It is disturbingly easy to make progress on the scales of attendance, building, and cash *even while failing to sustain significant conversation with God or enjoying redemptive relationships with people.* The program-based church may at times look great on paper. Its spiritual development, nevertheless, has been arrested halfway through Ezekiel's vision. God's call isn't merely that we assume appropriate forms, but that we become alive in the fullest sense of the word—filled and refilled with the Spirit of God, and therefore passionate about filling the world with lifelong learners of Jesus Christ. Consider the second part of Ezekiel's experience in the dry valley:

Then he said to me, "Prophesy to the breath; prophesy, son of man, and say to it, 'This is what the Sovereign Lord says: Come from the four winds, O breath, and breathe into these slain, that they may live.'" So I prophesied as he commanded me, and breath entered them; they came to life and stood up on their feet—a vast army.

Then he said to me, "Son of man, these bones are the whole house of Israel. They say, 'Our bones are dried up and our hope is gone; we are cut off.' Therefore prophesy and say to them: 'This is what the Sovereign Lord says: O my people, I am going to open your graves and bring you up from them; I will bring you back to the land of Israel. Then you, my people, will know that I am the Lord, when I open your graves and bring you up from them. I will put my Spirit in you and you will live...'" (Ez 37:9–14).

Learning How to Dance

When I was an eighth grader, our music teacher announced that our annual spring concert would feature selections from *The Sound of Music*. That was great news. She then indicated that a handful of singers would be specially featured up on stage in front of the whole school. The fact that my name was on her list was even better news. Then she spoke some of the most terrifying words I had ever heard. During one of the numbers the students up on stage would dance. With real partners. I would dance, with an actual girl, in front of people whose opinions mattered to me.

There are two main reasons I have never performed liturgical dance as part of a worship experience: my left foot and my right foot. I remember scientifically mastering the required steps for the dance number and practicing them at home, over and over again, in front of the family cat. Nothing ever felt so unnatural. Since I was the tallest boy I was paired with the tallest girl. On the day of the spring concert we stood together and joined hands, after which I faithfully executed the prescribed steps across the stage. But did I *dance*? Absolutely not.

There's a world of difference between knowing the right steps and knowing how to dance. There's a world of difference between structuring a church the right way and actually learning how to let go of the brakes—how to cease being fixated with programs and initiatives and Sunday morning bulletins, and simply to surrender to the movement of the Spirit, who causes our hearts to dance in the presence of God. It's the difference between the deadness of dry, institutional bones and authentic spiritual vitality.

The welcoming of God's Spirit is what separates a church that is focused on the maintenance of form from one that has genuinely heard and responded to the word of the Lord. The leaders of ABC churches prioritize survival and hunt for survival-enhancing programs. What is the next, best field-tested solution to the problems that we're facing? What new dance steps are on the market, and how exactly do we move our feet to pull off that pirouette? Real dancing, however, has far less to do with thinking about one's next move than simply feeling the music. Spirit-prompted congregations above all value a mission that is larger and vastly more important than their own organizational survival— bringing as many people as possible as far as possible down the pathway of imitating Jesus. Such churches intuitively understand that programs are not the answer. Instead they listen for Spirit-generated rhythms.

It's not that the ABCs of attendance, building, and cash suddenly become irrevlevant. Churches that are "in the Spirit" simply spend most of their time working, planning, and praying over *relation-ships*. It is their recurring experience that their most cherished goals are met as they help their members grow in their commitment to Christ as Lord; understand their identity as lifelong learners of Jesus; enter and sustain a relationship with a spiritual mentor; teach another person the basics of the Christian life; listen for God's voice in the context of a small group; and step out of their comfort zone in the realm of mission. Those are the relationships to which we will now turn.

It's time to say farewell to the ABC church. It's time to let go of the brakes. By the power of the Spirit we can go faster and farther than we've ever allowed ourselves to dream.

Questions for Further Exploration

Personal, one-on-one, or small groups

1. What is the history of your church? What was its original vision? How has that vision shifted in recent years? What percent of your members do you think could articulate your current vision?

2. Do you think that your church is a healthy place for leaders to lead? Why or why not?

3. If "10" means that your church is absorbed in addressing ABC issues, and "1" means that attendance, building, and cash are kept in proper perspective, how would you rate your congregation today? What evidence can you produce?

4. In what ways has church leadership grown your heart for God? How has being a church leader threatened your life with God?

5. The author makes a case that lay leaders need to receive permission to do authentic ministry. Do you agree? How could such permission be communicated?

Getting Started

On Your Own

"Hurry sickness" is an affliction of Western culture generally. In the church, over-scheduling and over-functioning are often applauded. Take a fearless personal inventory. As far as you can discern it, what is the boundary of God's call on your life? Where have you said "yes" when you should have said "no"? Determine this week to step back from every unnecessary commitment.

As a Congregation

Identify the chief issue or crisis that your church has faced in the areas of attendance, building, and cash over the past three years. How do these compare with the ABC issues that you are forecasting for the next three years? Identify the chief ways in which you moved forward in your church's overall vision during the past three years. What are the chief strategies in place to advance your vision during the next thirty-six months?

PART I

SIX DISCIPLING RELATIONSHIPS

When discerning the spiritual vitality of a particular church member, we all know the traditional questions: Do you regularly attend worship? Do you tithe? Are you active in Bible study? Are you helping the poor? These questions value a set of behaviors. While they are undoubtedly important, they cannot by themselves accomplish the work of spiritual transformation.

What if we asked a different set of questions? What would our churches look like if, more than anything, we valued a particular set of redemptive relationships?

The first part of this book will address a half-dozen such relationships from the perspective of the man who made the extraordinary shift from Christ-despiser to Christ-pursuer—the Pharisee named Saul of Tarsus, who became Paul the Christian missionary. How can we identify a healthy disciple, a lifelong learner of Jesus Christ? A disciple is someone who can answer, with ever-growing conviction and understanding, the following six questions:

Who is your Lord? When everything is said and done, whose agenda are you truly following?

Who are you? At the beginning of each day, do you wake up knowing that you'll have to go out and win your own share of security and significance, or can you truly say that those are priceless gifts you have already received?

Who is your Barnabas? Who is your spiritual mentor, the one from whom you are learning how to follow Jesus?

Who is your Timothy? Who is your apprentice, the one to whom you are passing along the lessons that God has entrusted to you?

Where is your Antioch? What small cadre of special friends is helping you to discern God's direction for your life?

Where is your Macedonia? What field of ministry is most closely aligned with God's call on your life and hauntingly stirs your deepest passion?

As we wrestle with these questions and seek God's answers to them, teaching others to do the same—our congregations will become different kinds of places. They will be healthier places. We will begin to measure success according to a different yardstick. We will surrender our futile quest to discover the one-size-fits-all program and grasp that God is powerfully and quietly at work within the mystery of discipling relationships.

WHO IS YOUR LORD?

To celebrate their fiftieth anniversary, my parents decided that they would host their own party. They invited their three sons and three daughters-in-law to join them on a Caribbean cruise in February. I don't recall agonizing for very long over the invitation. When someone hands you a free Get-Out-of-Indiana-in-February card, you take it. Speaking as veteran cruise passengers, my parents gushed, "We'll do all kinds of things together, and before dinner on the second day we'll even get a chance to stand in line and meet the captain." I rolled my eyes and said to Mary Sue, "Don't worry: I'll figure out a way to get us out of that one."

The trip was wonderful. Cruises are designed to be multisensory, it's-all-about-me experiences for the guests. At the end of the first evening of water-gazing and overindulging in the dining room we headed for bed. While we slept the boat quietly cruised out into the open water beyond Puerto Rico. At 4:48 a.m., however, everything changed. We were awakened by a disembodied voice on the cabin intercom.

"Ladies and gentlemen, this is your captain. I am very sorry to disturb you so early in the morning, but we have an urgent concern. We have an unconfirmed report that a passenger has fallen overboard. We have already turned the ship around and initiated a search." At that moment I realized for the first time that the boat was no longer moving. The captain continued, "Please go to your room if you are not there at this time, and account for everyone in your party. If anyone is missing, please report their name to the purser's desk immediately."

Thirty minutes passed. Through our window we could see searchlights sweeping across the swells of black water in the predawn darkness. The U.S. and Dutch Coast Guards had arrived on the scene. We found ourselves praying, "God, if anyone is out there alone in that ocean, may your mercy be upon him." The captain spoke a second time. "Ladies and gentlemen, two men are currently unaccounted for. Their names" [and here I will use fictional names] "are John Garcia and Eric Armstrong. If you know the whereabouts of either of these men please bring word to us right away."

There were 1,700 guests on the cruise boat and more than 700 crew members. From the list of 2,400 passengers the captain had narrowed the search to just two individuals. Fifteen minutes later he addressed us again. "Ladies and gentlemen, we are looking for Eric Armstrong." The energies of everyone on board were now focused on the hunt for a solitary person. Though he was a stranger to us, we all knew his name.

Two hours later the sun rose above the Caribbean. Once again we heard the captain's voice. "Ladies and gentlemen, I am very pleased to tell you we have just found Eric Armstrong. A U.S. Coast Guard helicopter is at this moment airlifting him to safety. He appears to be in good condition. Thank you for your cooperation during this time."

The successful search-and-rescue had a dramatic effect on the rest of the cruise. Every passenger now knew: *I'm sailing with someone who would turn this ship around in the middle of the night and come looking for me.* Who was Eric Armstrong? Was he a VIP…a U.S. Senator…the first mate…someone intimately related to the captain? No, he was a 20-year-old man who at about 4:30 a.m. was in a restricted area and had apparently fallen off the bow while doing "the Titanic thing"—*I'm king of the world!*

Before dinner on that second day there was no question what I wanted to do. I stood in line to meet the captain. I wanted to shake the hand of the man whom I knew would pull out all the stops to find one lost person, even someone who was doing the wrong thing at the wrong place at the wrong time.

It occurred to me later that this is precisely what Jesus did on the cross. He pulled out all the stops to launch a search-and-rescue for an entire world of lost people, a great many of whom remain oblivious to his very existence.

It's All about the Captain

If life is like a Caribbean cruise, then few contemporary Westerners would hesitate to affirm, "This trip is all about me. I am responsible to myself for having a wonderful time." In the midst of our self-discovery and self-indulgence, however, we continue to hear a persistent rumor circulating around the boat: The captain has performed heroically, even sacrificially, to guarantee our safety. It is therefore appropriate that the passengers express gratitude and acknowledgement from time to time. Otherwise, we are free to maintain our own schedules. The captain's job is to steer the boat. Ours is to enjoy the trip and stay out of trouble.

A fundamentally different picture, however, springs from the pages of Scripture. We owe everything to the captain. Therefore we are called to surrender our own agendas and to orient our lives around the captain's concerns. Our true status is not that of guests. We are called to sign on as mates. The trip is no longer all about us.

Our deepest satisfaction will lie in carrying out the captain's initiatives to serve our fellow passengers.

It's safe to say that perspective is a hard sell in twenty-first-century America. We much prefer being our own captain and cruise director. It's wonderful that the Man Up on the Bridge has provided for us—and we ought to be grateful, of course—but isn't it enough to stand in line and say thanks every now and then, after which we return to our own business?

The first and most important question for every human being concerns Lordship. *Who gets to be captain?* To what person or ideal have I given the authority to determine the agenda for the next twenty-four hours of my life? More than anything else, my answer to that question—not my well rehearsed got-my-Sunday-clothes-on religious answer, but the answer that is revealed by my actual behavior—is what determines the shape of my life.

Lordship in the World of Paul

The apostle Paul's preeminent concern was making a case for the Lordship of Jesus Christ. He considered "everything a loss compared to the surpassing greatness of knowing Christ Jesus my Lord, for whose sake I have lost all things" (Phil 3:8). The effect of Christ's death is that "all those who live should no longer live for themselves but for him who died for them and was raised again" (2 Cor 5:15). Lordship is decisive at the beginning of the Christian life: "That if you confess with your mouth, 'Jesus is Lord,' and believe in your heart that God raised him from the dead, you will be saved" (Rom 10:9). Lordship is also life's final goal: "that at the name of Jesus every knee should bow, in heaven and on earth and under the earth, and every tongue confess that Jesus Christ is Lord, to the glory of God the Father" (Phil 2:10,11).

In the first century it was no small matter to claim the Lordship of Jesus. During Paul's primary years of ministry the Roman Empire was in search of a unifying principle. Decades of conquest had left Rome with a vast conglomeration of nations, provinces, and tribes to oversee. Citizens of this far-flung empire had little in common. Ultimately the Romans concluded that a single act—a confession of loyalty once each year to the reigning Caesar—would guarantee that a male and his household were citizens in good standing.

The ritual was simple. All a man had to do was travel to an approved site, put a pinch of incense into the flame, and utter a two-word confession in the presence of witnesses: *Kaisar kurios.* "Caesar is Lord." The magistrate then issued him a *vitellus*—written certification of his obedience. The Romans themselves weren't exactly convinced that every Caesar was divine, especially in the case of deranged men like Caligula and Nero, whose reigns coincided with Paul's travels. In fact, an obedient citizen could say, "Caesar is Lord," and then go home to worship whatever god he chose.

Christians, however, could make only one confession: *Christos kurios.* "Christ is Lord." Even when magistrates suggested helpfully, "Just speak the words of loyalty to the Empire," Christians dissented by the thousands. Depending on the leadership of the day, that disobedience might mean torture and death. An exasperated Pliny, having failed to persuade numerous Christians to affirm the Lordship of Caesar and curse the name of Christ, wrote, "None of these acts, it is said, those who are really Christians can be compelled to do."

With regard to publicly claiming his name, Jesus reserved some of his strongest comments for those who got the words right, but whose hearts remained on a different wavelength. "Why do you call me, 'Lord, Lord,' and do not do what I say?" (Lk 6:46). In his book, *The Soul's Quest for God*, theologian R.C. Sproul notes the significance of *double address* in both Old and New Testaments. Calling someone's name twice was a way of speaking forcefully, emotionally, and even intimately. (Tyndale, 1992, p.220f). As the flint knife hovered above Isaac, the angel called, "Abraham, Abraham."

At the burning bush God said, "Moses, Moses." The young boy trying to sleep in the tabernacle kept hearing God's wooing voice: "Samuel, Samuel." Jesus cried out on the cross, "My God, my God, why have you forsaken me?" And a notorious lyncher of Christians was summoned to a new life with the words, "Saul, Saul, why do you persecute me?"

If you wanted to reach deep down into somebody's soul, speak his or her name twice. It was a way of saying, "This is not third-class mail. You are not being telemarketed. *I know who you are.*" Against that background Jesus says, "How dare you say to me, 'Lord, Lord'—implying that you and I are best friends—when your behavior proves that we don't really know each other at all?"

Lordship on His Terms

American churches are filled with constituents who claim some degree of intimacy with Jesus. Our first task—and it is not an easy one—is to challenge those who have no idea what they're saying when the words, "Lord, Lord," come out of their mouths.

I used to do theological jousting with a pastor who had some nontraditional ideas about God's character and activity in the world. I think he had personally invented a good deal of what he believed. When I pressed him on some of the details, and intimated that conjuring up his own religion wasn't the wisest course, he would smile and say, "God and I have an understanding."

According to Jesus, we do indeed need to come to an understanding with God—based not on *our terms*, but on *his terms*. Jesus goes on in Luke 6:47–49 to say that two things are true of every person. Every one of us is building a life. And every one of our personal building projects is going to be put to the test. We're all building a "house" that represents the entirety of our existence, and every house in the human subdivision is going to be struck squarely by the spiritual equivalent of Hurricane Andrew. Whose house is going to stand?

Jesus is blunt. The person who hears his words and puts them into practice is like a builder who digs down deep and lays his foundation on bedrock. The person who hears but doesn't obey—who chooses to follow a personalized agenda or clings to the promises of a different "lord"—is headed for disaster.

The words of Luke 6:46–49 are meant to be frightening. Their intent is to scare us out of whatever complacent assumptions we have made concerning the Lordship of Christ. We cannot say, "Oh, it's OK. God and I have an understanding." The truth is that Jesus calls us to obey him as Lord—as he understands that term. What are our possible responses?

In Search of an Alternative Lord

One option is to go searching for a different Lord. The alternatives are limitless. Someone or something has to function as the master of our lives. All people are security-seekers. That's simply the way that human beings are wired. But where shall we seek ultimate security? Shall we seek it in things or in God— in what is created, or in the one who created them? That's where we discover who or what is functioning as our Lord.

At one point in her career pop singer Madonna was interviewed in London about her personal spirituality. Here's an excerpt from Andrew Neil's feature in *The Sunday Times*, as included in Vaughan Roberts' book, *Turning Points*:

> Q: "When you gathered your dancers around you during the "Blond Ambition" tour to pray before going on stage, who were you praying to?"
> A: "Who was I praying to?" She repeats the question, stalling for time. "Everyone in the room and my idea of God."

27

Q: "Is there a god?"

A: "Yes," she replied quickly. "There's my god. Every-one has their own god."

Q: "Tell me about him."

A: "I can't describe it."

Q: "You have a good idea though?"

A: "Yes." The voice was strained quiet. "To me, some-times, I don't know if it's a being or more like the highest state of my consciousness, like trying to rise above everyday life and the things that bring you down, and mortality and things like that...It's like calling on any power I have inside myself. It's a protector, an advisor; it's soothing, comforting...and non-judgmental."

Q: "But is it a supreme being?"

A: "I don't know. You know I really have unformed ideas about it because I could change my mind in about half an hour. I think religion should be a very personal thing. It's what you get your strength from."

Q: "So it's an inner matter rather than an organized religion?"

A: "Yeah, I think." By this time she was almost whis-pering.

(OM Publishing, 1999, pp. 48–49)

It may seem comforting to "own" a spirituality that can be ad-justed every half hour. But, as Paul asserts in Romans 1:18–25, hu-man beings eventually choose to bow before something that makes claims of absolute authority.

The Cathedral of Notre Dame stands in the oldest part of Paris, on a large island in the middle of the Seine River. For the past nine hundred years its soaring towers, flying buttresses, exotic gargoyles and stained-glass rose windows have dramatically represented for the people of Paris the primacy of the worship of God.

During a brief season, however, something else was worshipped within the walls of Notre Dame. In 1793, just seventeen years after the launching of the American Revolution, Christianity was openly rejected by the leaders of the French Revolution. More than 1,400 city streets were renamed in an effort to erase the memories of church history. The cathedral itself was proclaimed to be the Temple of Reason. A huge papier-mâché mountain covered with pagan symbols was constructed in the sanctuary. A local actress was hired to play the role of Liberty. Dressed in a white robe, she dramatically bowed before the flame of reason, then seated herself on a bank of plants and flowers. Those present worshipfully put their faith in the ultimate value of human reason.

Now, we may congratulate ourselves for never having bowed before a papier-mâché mountain covered with pagan symbols; but if we aren't proclaiming and living out the Lordship of Christ, we are certainly worshipping something else. If the words of Jesus aren't where we are seeking absolute security, we will inevitably "absolutize" something else and live every day as if that is where security can be found.

Possessions, Pleasures, and Power

American culture has unapologetically absolutized—that is, made more important than anything else—*possessions, pleasures and power*. The highest values of our society are having nice stuff, having a good time, and having control—feeling good, looking good, and making good. Thomas Gillespie, president of Princeton Theological Seminary, says that we live in a carnival atmosphere where sideshow barkers are continually beckoning us. Step right up. Here's the security you've been looking for. Buy this car and you'll feel free. Purchase these toys and your kids will stop complaining. Use this perfume and you'll be lovable, adorable, and worthy of being touched. Gargle with this mouthwash and people will enjoy being in your presence.

Why do these sideshow strategies appear to work? It's because they are pitched toward our deepest, security-seeking impulses— the ones that God graciously planted within us as "homing beacons." God alone is the provider of absolute security. Our deepest yearnings are fulfilled when the true Lord assumes his rightful role in our lives. Crowning a false lord who makes less arduous demands —in other words, absolutizing anything less than Christ—is a formula for spiritual shipwreck.

Does our culture really pretend that possessions, pleasures, and powers have as much validity as the gospel? Christianity and commercial advertisers are clearly in direct competition. A cell phone provider claims that you can "rule the world from your cubicle," and that their product is "how to get life done." "How can you make two months' salary last forever?" That does sound like an inscrutable problem, but never forget that, just like God, "a diamond is forever." God may promise new life, but a brand of men's hair coloring is "the rejuvenator." A remarkable golf club is able to impart "exceptional forgiveness."

Now let's be honest. This is false advertising. Technology is not worthy of our deepest trust. Opening a new IRA does not bring ultimate satisfaction. Real life is not a beach. Here's how Jesus put it: "What does it profit somebody to gain the whole world, yet lose his own soul?" (Mt 16:26). Our culture has gambled that the accumulation of titles and toys is the key to life's meaning. Our culture has gambled, and it will lose big.

The Antidote to Worry

Jesus says, "Don't worry, saying, 'What shall we eat?' or 'What shall we drink?' or 'What shall we wear?'" Five times in Matthew 6:25–34 Jesus confronts worry. What is worry? It begins with fear—fear that things aren't going to work out for us, that our personal dreams are in danger of being derailed, that our deepest needs for love and acceptance and security might not be met. Therefore we have to find our own Lord. We have to be our own Lord. I like this definition of worry: fear that has unpacked its bags and decided to stay for a while. Chronic worry is fear that has signed a 30-year mortgage and declared, "You can't live without me, can you?"

Jesus says that worry is unwarranted. Why? He observes that pagans—people who have opted to obey another lord—are obsessed with the meeting of their own needs. But God the Father knows our needs and will take care of us. He summarizes our best option in Matthew 6:33: "But seek first his kingdom and his righteousness, and all these things will be given to you as well."

What would it be like to populate a church with men and women who are betting their lives that that statement is true? It would mean that outsiders would be able to look at us and say, "Life under the Lordship of Jesus does indeed look different." Our silly game playing could finally come to an end. We could arrive at church without fixing our hair just so and not die. We could wear the same necktie two weeks in a row and not feel stupid. We could agree that our teenage girls don't have to look like skinny models to be beautiful—that they don't have to starve themselves to death trying to achieve what doesn't matter. We could realize that we don't need to own things to enjoy things. Our fanaticism to hold and to clutch could give way to sharing and to sacrificing.

What if those who said, "Lord, Lord," to Jesus also chose to let Jesus establish their agenda? Pastors wouldn't need to invest hours trying to persuade already-busy parishioners to do a bit of volunteering. "Commitment" wouldn't be an annual deployment of new strategies designed to capture the calendar, wallet, and thought life of unsuspecting or resistant church members. Could such an environment really exist? Of course it could—on the other side of a widely shared, radical commitment. The only way to escape the lie that the good life comes down to looking good, feeling good, and making good is for a community of disciples to agree that the Lordship of Jesus is the only real good.

Can We Renegotiate?

The classic church strategy, naturally, is not to seek another lord (at least consciously), but to renegotiate Jesus' terms. Maybe he isn't entirely serious. Maybe we can retain a significant gap between what we proclaim and what we do.

In truth, the issue is whether we ourselves are *living* out the principles that we are willing to *talk* about in the presence of others. To claim the words, "Lord, Lord," concerning Christ, implying that he is the one with whom we have a transforming, intimate relationship, is to put ourselves on the spot. Are we living models of everything that Jesus taught? If not, why not? Does our gap exist in the realm of knowing what he taught, understanding what he taught, or trusting what he taught? How shall we close those gaps?

The most tempting tactic is to invent and proclaim a picture of Jesus that is suspiciously accommodated to our current level of obedience. Perhaps church bulletins should come with a disclaimer: Any connection between today's sermon and real characters from the New Testament is entirely unintended.

When we go to the movies, we've all learned to suspend judgment about what we're seeing. Hollywood is most certainly not a window on the real world. Film critic Roger Ebert notes that movies consistently make and follow their own rules. The average cop, for example, is required to shoot several people a week just to solve problems. Every time someone leaves a grocery store there has to be a loaf of French bread sticking out the top of the bag—even though few of us ever buy unwrapped French bread. Whenever a man and a woman are running from danger, he always grabs her hand—even though it's obvious that people holding hands run more slowly. Whenever a man is viciously beaten up he shows no pain, but whenever a woman tries to clean his wounds, he is required to wince. In Hollywood you can pick any lock in a matter of seconds with a credit card or a paper clip, or just kick right through a dead bolt lock—unless, of course, the building is on fire and there is a child trapped inside.

At the movies, we've all learned to suspend judgment. This isn't the way the world actually works. If only Christians applied the same kind of discernment to what we so often see and hear in church: Who is Jesus? He's the advocate for our way of life. He comes to us promising that our businesses will make lots of money if only we do a little Bible study every week. He assures us that if families pray together, they will never suffer major problems. If we give away a bit of our discretionary income, we don't have to think seriously about the poor. Jesus' main mission is to comfort us and to fulfill our dreams. Jesus is here to make us happy.

Leo Tolstoy points out that every person has to choose between two Gods. Most people opt for "the God who is here to serve me." The difficulty, as Tolstoy reminds us, is that such a God doesn't exist. Clinging to the expectation that Christ exists to make me happy is a recipe for deep disappointment. Why doesn't he give me what I want? Why doesn't he make things better? (as cited by Dallas Willard, *The Renovation of the Heart*, Navpress 2002, p. 40).

Alive to Do What Jesus Wants

Tolstoy's alternative is the God whom I myself am called to serve, with all my heart, mind, soul, and strength. The Lordship of Jesus means waking up with the conviction that we have received the gift of life in order to do what Jesus wants. The cruise is not all about us. It's all about the captain.

What do we do with such a statement? We take it with us, wherever we go, for weeks and months at a time. We ask for the Holy

Spirit's help and we reflect upon it—seriously and courageously. "I am alive to do what Jesus wants." What does Jesus want? Jesus wants justice. How therefore should I help bring about economic justice in a world where the haves and the have-nots are growing further and further apart? Jesus wants truth. How do I speak the truth when everybody else is lying to cover up our firm's bad business practices? Jesus wants reconciliation. How do I take the first step to make things right in those relationships where everything feels wrong?

The more we study Scripture and the more we reflect with other Christians, the better we will become at identifying what we need to be thinking about. To see the world as Christ sees the world, we will need to ponder the fact that people live forever...that if our Lord indeed rules the universe, there are no accidents or coincidences...that because this moment counts, what we're about to do or think or say will have eternal significance. Faithfulness in following Jesus may be defined as progressively closing the gap between *who we really are* and *who Jesus really is*—not the fictional Jesus who is conveniently adjusted to our behavior, but one before whom every knee shall one day bow.

In an article in the December 1980 issue of *Proclaim* magazine, Brian Harbour told the story of Bill Rittinghouse who, many years before, was driving through Kansas. As a heavily loaded station wagon passed him, Rittinghouse noticed that a suitcase strapped to the roof was working itself loose. It suddenly fell from the back of the wagon, hit the road, then bounced onto the shoulder. Rittinghouse sped up to try to signal the driver of the wagon, but failed. When he opened the suitcase he found clothing, some personal items, and a small white box with a rubber band around it. Inside was a wad of cotton that cushioned a $20 gold piece. On one side it said, "Twenty years loyal and faithful service." On the other side was printed, "Presented to Otis Sampson by the Northwestern

States Portland Cement Company." Otis shouldn't be too hard to find, Rittinghouse thought.

The search proved to be difficult, however. After contacting seventy-five different cities in the American Northwest he finally found the cement company. "Yes, we know Otis Sampson. He used to work here. Would you like his forwarding number?" When Rittinghouse placed the call, Otis was ecstatic. "You can keep everything else in the suitcase," he said. "But please send me the $20 gold piece. It's my most precious possession."

As Rittinghouse boxed up the coin he decided he would include a personal letter. It described his World War II adventures— his escape from a Romanian prison and his calling out to God for help. He told how his family had decided to become Christians, and exactly what it meant to know Christ. "In fact," he wrote, "I can truthfully say that my relationship with Jesus is my most prized possession." And he mailed the letter.

More than a year went by. Rittinghouse assumed he would never again hear from Otis Sampson. But at Christmas he received a small box in the mail. Inside were the same $20 gold piece and a personal note. Otis had written, "Last Sunday my wife and I were baptized in a little church here in Colorado. We are two old people. I'm seventy-four years old and she's seventy-two. We want you to have the gold piece to carry with you at all times. You were the first one to tell us of Jesus Christ. Now he is our most precious possession."

Discipleship begins with a question: Who is your Lord? What is your most prized possession? Exchanging what we used to trust for security and significance for a relationship with Jesus Christ is the one true doorway to the adventure that awaits us.

Questions for Further Exploration

Personal, one-on-one, or small groups

1. "My life is all about me." Would you agree that this statement accurately describes current Western culture? What evidence have you seen this week?

2. If your unchurched neighbors studied your church, where would they see evidence of the Lordship of Jesus? Where do you think they would see a gap between what your church claims and how it actually lives?

3. What do leaders and members of your church tend to worry about? How would a fuller surrender to Christ change this?

4. What do you personally tend to worry about? In what areas of your life are you still attempting to maintain control?

5. What aspect of complete personal surrender to the leadership of Christ fills you with the most apprehension? What has prevented you from taking this step?

Getting Started

On Your Own

Set aside a lengthy period of time for solitude and reflection. Search your own heart and ask these questions: What am I counting on to make me happy? What am I hoping for above everything else? What is the last personal dream that I am willing to surrender? Ask God to give you a clear picture of the fulfillment that comes from counting on Jesus...and nothing else. Take the statement, "I am alive to do what Jesus wants," wherever you go, in every situation, for the next week. Share with someone else what you learned at the end of that time.

As a Congregation

Jesus said, "Why do you call me, 'Lord, Lord,' but do not do what I say?" (Lk 6:46). The busyness of the contemporary church—our sheer level of distraction—often clouds our ability to see the totality of Christ's call. Make a list of at least three things that Jesus has commanded that are not receiving sufficient priority in the life of your church. Discuss openly why this is true. Be bold and be specific, remembering that the mercy of Christ is beyond measure.

Now: *What do you intend to do?*

WHO ARE YOU?

A number of years ago a little girl on the East Coast made the following statement: "My name is Martha Bowers Taft. My great-grandfather was President of the United States. My grandfather was a United States Senator. My daddy is ambassador to Ireland. And I am a Brownie."

That little girl was very fortunate. She knew exactly who she was. If life's most important question is, "Who's in charge?" then life's second most important question is, "What's my relationship to the one who's in charge?" The New Testament empowers every Christian to give this answer: "My Lord is master of the universe. His Father is the creator and sustainer of everything. And I am his deeply loved servant and disciple."

How do we apply to get this identity? It's not that big a deal, really. All we have to do is start life over again. As Vaughan Roberts points out in *Turning Points*, Jesus' assertion that we must be born again is not exactly a compliment. (OM Publishing, 1999, p. 151).

Consider the likelihood of my becoming a starter in the National Football League. In central Indiana it's definitely cool to be an Indianapolis Colt. OK, from time to time it's somewhat cool to be an Indianapolis Colt. Suppose I were to work myself into condition and arrange for a private tryout with my local pro team. Afterward I'd approach the Colts' coaching staff and say, "Now don't sugar-coat it. Just talk to me straight. What are my chances of being on the field this fall?" And the coaches would say something like, "McDonald, the only way you'll end up playing for this franchise is by being born again." Literally. Different chromosomes. A father who was a Bulgarian wrestling champion. A mother who was…well, a Bulgarian wrestling champion. Add to that a lifestyle based on actual regular exercise, and I may have a shot.

When Jesus says that his followers must be spiritually reborn, he's saying that we have no realistic chance of participating in his vision for the future unless we start over again with a new vision, new capacities, new motivation, and an entirely new nature that is capable of responding positively to God.

A Whole New Identity

No spiritual rebirth has been more celebrated or scrutinized than that of Saul of Tarsus, whose first step to becoming Paul the Christian missionary required a blinding, spiritual knock-down on the road to Damascus. Paul never got over this dramatic change of identity. Even at the end of life he was still amazed that God could transform a misguided, murderous zealot.

Prior to conversion Paul sported impeccable spiritual credentials in the eyes of his Jewish contemporaries and had the perfect Sabbath attendance pins to prove it. In Philippians 3:4 he writes, "If anyone else thinks he has reasons to put confidence in the flesh, I have more: circumcised on the eighth day, of the people of Israel, of the tribe of Benjamin, a Hebrew of Hebrews; in regard to the law, a Pharisee; as for zeal, persecuting the church; as for legalistic righteousness, faultless." In Acts 22:3 Paul adds, "under Gamaliel

I was thoroughly trained in the law of our fathers..." This would be like a physicist recalling that he was Albert Einstein's graduate assistant. Paul was everything a first century Jewish mother could ever dream.

Meeting Christ—or rather, being met by Christ in mid-step—turned everything on its head. "But whatever was to my profit I now consider loss for the sake of Christ...I consider them rubbish" (a gracious translation, since the Greek clearly means "excrement") "that I may gain Christ and be found in him, not having a righteousness of my own that comes from the law, but that which is through faith in Christ..."(Phil 3:7–9). Paul's identity changed from spiritual super-achiever to "*doulos* of Christ," which is the way he introduces himself at numerous junctures, including the opening of his letters to both the Romans and the Philippians.

A Call to Servanthood

In most English versions of the Bible there are two words that describe how someone might relate to a master or lord: "servant" or "slave." Both words, however, turn out to be translations of the very same Greek word: *doulos*. In Scripture every slave is a servant and every servant is a slave. Jesus invites us to choose a voluntary enslavement to him as our permanent way of life.

What kind of choice is that? Slavery is one of the most reprehensible concepts in the modern world. Slavery is what we wish had *never* been part of this nation's history. It's important to note, however, that there are significant differences between chattel slavery as it came to be practiced in the New World and the slavery that existed in the Mediterranean world of the first century. Within the Roman Empire, approximately one-third of the population were slaves. Another one-third of the population were *freed* slaves. As Brian Dodd observes in *The Problem with Paul*, there is no record of a freed slave championing the cause of eradicating slavery itself.

41

Certainly one of the reasons for such silence is that slavery had become a very good thing for many people. (InterVarsity Press, 1996, p. 82)

While many African slaves in America were subjected to brutality and humiliation, numerous slaves in the time of Paul enjoyed productive and contented lives. American slaves generally had no rights, no property, and little hope for the future. But many slaves in Bible times were highly educated, often more so than anyone else in the households they served. Ancient world slaves were of diverse races and backgrounds. Most importantly, many of them had actually chosen to become slaves. They saw slavery as an opportunity to advance their own interests. *That's because honor and status were associated with being the slave of an honorable master.*

We may be confident that Paul would have taken little delight in saying, "I am a slave. *Period.*" What filled his heart with joy was being able to declare, "I know who I am. I am a slave—a slave *of Christ.*" To be Christ's servant/slave is to be affiliated with the most important person in the cosmos, and thus to be granted the highest possible honor.

The Honor Game, Then and Now

It's hard to overstate the importance of honor in the ancient Near East. The Honor Game is alive and well in our time, to be sure, but only superficially. Who tends to receive recognition and "positive buzz" today? Extraordinary individuals. Beautiful people. Those who make the list of Barbara Walters' "Ten Most Interesting Interviews." Celebrities—people who are famous chiefly for being famous. Sports stars. Notorious criminals. The man who can eat more pitted prunes in one hour than anyone else, thus earning a spot in the *Guinness Book of World Records*. Winners of the local Honor Game are those who earn the best grades, hit the most jump shots, date the neatest guys, set the loftiest sales records, and grow the most beautiful begonias.

In Bible times things were different. Honor was identified neither with celebrity nor notoriety. Instead it was a measurement of one's public standing and worthiness to receive respect. Honor was the most valuable social commodity in the first century. From certain perspectives it was more precious than life itself. Honor meant reputation. It meant security. Honor is why Joseph is celebrated for protecting his fiancée's reputation, even after discovering that Mary was pregnant. Money might be nice, but why make money unless it could bring honor? Ominously, it was agreed by all that honor was a limited commodity. There was never enough to go around. If one person obtained greater honor it was only because somebody else had tragically or foolishly forfeited their share.

If the pursuit of honor was a chief fixation of the Greeks, the Romans, and the Jews, how did they figure that an individual might make progress? Honor did not come by being clever or smart or blessed with superlative DNA. Honor came by entering a relationship with a highly important person.

In the ancient world such a person was a called a patron. A patron was typically the head of a "household," which could have several hundred members. A large household would likely include relatives and slaves and numerous outsiders who were continually attempting to "get ahead" or to increase their public stock by presenting themselves as very important associates of the patron. Here we see the origin of the term "patronage."

An example of how patronage works comes from the early days of the American film industry. Before "Wild Bill" Wellman became one of Hollywood's legendary directors, he was essentially a nobody hanging around studio sets trying to get noticed. Few paid attention to him. One day, "Black Jack" Pershing, America's most famous World War I general, dropped by the outdoor film set where Wellman was running errands. Wellman had fought in the trenches with Pershing, and the general recognized and admired him. "Bill," he said, "let me know if there's anything I can ever do for you." "General," said Wellman, "would you be willing to walk with me over to that tree, and then just stand there with me for a while so that I could look important?" The very next day Bill Wellman, who was now The Friend of General Pershing, got the Hollywood job that launched his career.

Who are you? What relationship, achievement, or stroke of luck are you counting on to define your identity? Paul chose to lose the Honor Game that was so highly valued by his own people, the one that was based on titles and achievements, even though halfway through the race he was six lengths ahead of everybody else. Paul gladly embraced a new identity—lifelong servant/slave of a crucified carpenter.

The same identity is available to us. Our call is to seek honor not in personal triumphs or beauty or bucks, but by placing ourselves at the disposal of Jesus Christ, the *Most Important Person* and most honorable master in the universe. To do that will always mean losing face. It will always mean, from the perspective of our culture, that we are foolishly sacrificing our competitive edge in the Honor Game. And that takes courage.

Jesus himself showed the way. Given the opportunity to define his own identity, Jesus declared, "For even the Son of Man did not come to be served, but to serve, and to give his life as a ransom for many" (Mk 10:45). Paul writes that Jesus "did not consider equality with God something to be grasped, but made himself nothing, taking the very nature of a servant" (Phil 2:6,7). Furthermore, as Paul and countless other Christ-followers can testify, the old saying turns out to be true: The quickest way to the throne room is through the servant's entrance. For God's Son and for God's most trusted agents, servanthood is the only way forward.

Changing Our Name and Changing Our Game

That's not to say that claiming a servant's identity and excelling at servanthood are the same thing. In the spring of 2000, Dickie Simpkins, back-up point guard for the badly outgunned Chicago Bulls, noticed one evening that his own team had misspelled his name on his new basketball jersey. The letters "m" and "i" had been switched. Instead of being Dickie Simpkins he was now Dickie Smipkins.

Simpkins went out that night and played the best NBA game of his career. It was as if he couldn't miss. Superstitiously he decided to change the spelling on all of his Bulls' jerseys. Now playing as Dickie Smipkins, he tore up the league for more than a week, leading the Bulls to three consecutive victories. Then reality struck. Smipkins started playing like Simpkins again and the Bulls sank back to the NBA cellar. What's the moral of the story? There's a whale of a difference between changing your name and changing your game.

One of the responsibilities for those who lead a Spirit-filled congregation is to propose name changes for the back of everyone's jersey. In a healthy church we must regularly affirm that every individual is called to be servant, not just a spectator of church life. Our call is to be *worshipper of God*, seven days a week, 24 hours a day—not just an attender of church services. Every woman and man is furthermore called to be *care-giver*, not just an end user of God's grace and mercy. Likewise our jerseys ought to say *missionary*—right where we are, right where we already live and work and play—so that we don't settle for being senders of somebody else into God's world. What's the catch with all these changes of identity? There's a whale of difference between changing our church names and changing our games.

How do these shifts become a reality? Not by faking it. Not by trying harder. It may be admirable to vow, "From now on I'm going to act like and think like a faithful servant," but we won't get far. We don't have the heart for it. Remember the words of Jesus: "You must be born again" (Jn 3:3). Turning away from the bankruptcy of false lords and embracing the Lordship of Jesus is where we begin. Spiritual renewal provides the equivalent of a heart transplant. Then God graciously pours the Holy Spirit into our hearts. The Spirit is the one who transforms us, through daily promptings, reminders, and encouragements, into men and women who are increasingly able to join young Samuel in saying, "Speak, Lord, for your servant is listening" (1 Sm 3:10).

Intentional Imitators

Let's return to that statement of identity that is ours through God's grace: "I am a deeply loved servant and *disciple* of my Lord." What does it mean to be a disciple?

A disciple is a lifelong learner...an intentional imitator...a spiritual apprentice...a lifelong pursuer of the real and only life...a forever student in the school of Jesus Christ. Being a disciple of Jesus means intentionally presenting our selves to Christ every day, so that our thoughts, words, actions, and motives might gradually become more like his. In later chapters we will explore the challenges and realities of such a disciple life in detail.

Who is qualified to follow this path? Who is sufficiently gifted and motivated to self-enroll in the college of spiritual growth? The word *disciple*, unfortunately, has all too often been used by recent generations as if it were a synonym for "super-Christian." Some fellowships have even taught that discipleship is optional—a graduate level course for unusually zealous men and women.

All the evidence from the New Testament, however, is that Jesus issued only one call to humanity—a call to a life of absolute dependence on him. A disciple isn't someone who has achieved a certain level of maturity, but a student who has enrolled in becoming like

Christ. First graders may have a long way to go before receiving a bachelor's degree, but they definitely qualify as committed learners. It's not how far we've gone down the path. What matters is our commitment to being a lifelong path-follower.

There is no higher proof of that than the glimpses that Scripture provides of Jesus' twelve original disciples. It's astonishing to contemplate the kind of people to whom he was willing to entrust the spiritual future of the human race. By the time the Twelve had gathered with Jesus at the Last Supper—following at least three years of intensive training and partnership with the Son of God—what we see is an inspiring display of spiritual maturity. *OK, not exactly*.

Slow Learners

On the way to the upper room James and John became embroiled in a nasty spat with the rest of the disciples. Jesus had nicknamed these two sibling fishermen "Boanerges," or "sons of thunder," which in today's parlance might roughly translate as Bomb Heads. They had audaciously announced their ambition to secure spots #1 and #2 in the kingdom of God. For all they cared, everyone else could finish in a tie for third place. Servanthood was the least of the identities they craved.

Somewhere at that table in the upper room sat Matthew, who before joining the band of disciples worked as a tax collector. Essentially that meant Matthew had earned his living as a professional thief through a kind of government-endorsed extortion. Simon the Zealot was the Twelve's resident terrorist. The Zealots were nobody's fools. They were passionately committed to overturning their current political situation—the rule of the Roman Empire—and would bring it about by force if that became necessary. The Zealots weren't exactly committed to a strategy of prayer meetings.

Thomas and Philip were the two disciples with the questions and the doubts. In John 14 we learn that at the Last Supper Philip was confused. "'Lord, show us the Father and that will be enough for us.' Jesus answered, 'Don't you know me, Philip, even after I have been among you such a long time? Anyone who has seen me has seen the Father. How can you say, 'Show us the Father'?" Thomas of course was the disciple who on Easter Sunday would say, "*Show me the Miracle*. Until I see it with my own eyes I won't believe that Jesus is alive" (Jn 20:25).

Simon Peter was the identified leader of the Twelve. He was a man of extremes, with Himalayan highs and off-the-chart lows. He loved Jesus and he failed Jesus. He was the first to recognize Jesus' true identity, then the first one to say, "Lord, you're not going to sacrifice yourself, are you? That would ruin everything!" *Get behind me, Satan*, Jesus said to Peter's face at that moment (Mt 16:16–23). This we know for sure: At the time of the Last Supper, Peter was still ricocheting between the extremes. Within a few hours he made absolute promises of loyalty, then made an absolute fool of himself by swearing three times that Jesus and he were not so much as acquaintances.

And what about the host in the upper room? Jesus looked around that table of people with their deeply embedded competitiveness, their secret spiritual betrayal, their persistent doubts, and their certainty that might would make right, and he prayed, "Father, as you sent me into the world, now I have sent them into the world" (Jn 17:6). Eleven slow learners were about to be turned loose on the rest of humanity. "Go recruit others, too," Jesus commanded them. History has proved that ordinary people who have enrolled themselves as lifetime spiritual imitators—even when bearing evident shortcomings and flaws—can indeed be extraordinary disciples.

Loved by God

Who are you? There is a final and crucial component to a Christian's identity: "I am a *deeply loved* servant and disciple of my Lord."

What is the most important common noun in the New Testament? It is *love*. God is love. Love bears all things, believes all things, hopes all things, endures all things (1 Cor 13:7, KJV).

What is the most important verb in the New Testament? It is *love*. Jesus' greatest commandment is to love God for all we're worth, and his second greatest commandment is to love people with equal passion. "For God so loved the world…" that God the Son moved heaven and earth to rescue us (Jn 3:16).

Nevertheless, my distinct impression is that few churchgoers, when asked, "Who are you…*really?*" would unhesitatingly answer, "I am someone who is infinitely loved by God." Oh, sure, we reason, God loves us because he has to. He is theologically obligated. But he probably doesn't want to. And we wouldn't be altogether shocked if God announced that he finds us very challenging to like. God's acceptance is not easy to accept, especially when "I ought to be ashamed of myself" feels more natural than "I am worthy of being loved."

What is shame? It is a pervasive feeling that I am not the person that I should be, and that I can't wriggle out of the mess that I've gotten myself into. As Lewis Smedes puts it in his book *Shame and Grace*, "The feeling of shame is about our very *selves*, not about some bad thing we *did* or *said* but about what we *are*. It tells us that we *are* unworthy. Totally. We feel that we *are* unacceptable."

Shame can be healthy, of course. It can be a God-given realization that there is a gap between where I stand right now and where God wants me to be. Healthy shame is a call back to the life that God wants me to pursue.

Theoretically our experience of shame should be over as soon as we accept the Lordship of the one who loves us. But for far too many of us, the heaviness never seems to go away. We get stuck in the muck and the mire of unhealthy shame—the feeling that because of who we are, things are never going to be right. Smedes continues:

> *Shame can fall over you when a person stares at you after you've said something inane at a party, or when you think everyone is clucking at how skinny or how fat or how clumsy you are. It comes when no one else is looking at you but yourself and what you see is a phony, a coward, a bore, a failure, a dumbbell, a person whose nose is too big and whose legs are too bony, or a mother who is incompetent at mothering, and, all in all, a poor dope with little hope of ever becoming an acceptable human being.*

(HarperSanFrancisco, 1993, p.6)

Forgiven and Accepted

Unhealthy shame is all about alleged evidence that I am a black sheep in the family of God. It declares that I am unacceptable as a human being. I am not worthy of being loved. Such a feeling is obviously the antithesis of God's declarations that I am God's child (Jn 1:12), Christ's friend (Jn 15:15), a member of Christ's body (I Cor 12:27), have been bought with a price (I Cor 6:19,20), and am complete in Christ (Col 2:10).

Unhealthy shame is what turns people's eyes away from God's accepting gaze and toward the arbitrary ideals of other people. I know a woman who can hardly write a personal note because she is tormented by the thought that its recipient will undoubtedly read it and judge it to be awkward, foolish, and insincere. This intelligent woman feels stupid and paralyzed as she holds a pen over a blank piece of paper.

Smedes points out that unhealthy shame clings to overly responsible people—those who have the good sense to realize that the world is filled with pain, but the misguided sense that it is their job to fix it (*Shame and Grace*, p. 18). When they fail, they feel devastated. Early in my ministry I got a phone call from someone who said, "Glenn, you really need to go visit Mr. Smith," who was an elderly gentleman I knew. "He's asking a lot of spiritual questions." But I was very tired and very busy, and the day I got that phone call I didn't make time to visit Mr. Smith. Late that night he died. How could I live with myself? No one was there to address his spiritual questions *on the day he died*. Unhealthy shame wraps itself around us when we forget that it is God who has the whole world in his hands. It is God who says, "Please keep on living. Entrust your friend to me. I'm in charge of the universe."

Sadly, church can be a place where many of us experience the full effects of not-good-enoughness. Sometimes it's because a congregation doesn't know how to communicate grace, and sometimes it's because of the baggage that we bring with us. I know that every time I challenge our flock concerning the six marks of a disciple, there is a certain percentage of the crowd that sighs, "Well, thank you very much. Now I have a half dozen more reasons to feel like a failure."

Our call is to think like Jesus and talk like Jesus and be like Jesus. But in truth the vast majority of us have extended periods of time when we don't want to be anything like that at all. Maybe we sit in church and daydream about punching out an irritating relative, or wishing that a business rival would be caught cheating, or hoping that we could pursue forbidden sexual adventures, or running away from our aging parents who are depending on us, or simply wishing that life would hurry up and end so we don't have to feel so much pain. Then when it's time to pray we think, "As if...as if God could possibly reach down and love me right now, since he knows all about the sewer of my imagination." Thus we conclude that we're not worthy of being called, or commissioned, or adored, or accepted, or any of those other words we're likely to hear from the pulpit.

The Truth That Makes Us Free

What in the world can we do? Smedes says it best: "What we have to do is address the lies that we tell ourselves. Nobody gets up in the morning and says, 'Boy, I think I'll tell myself a whopper of a lie today...and then believe it.' But that's standard behavior for all too many of God's children. We believe the lie that we have to make ourselves acceptable before we can be accepted, and our feelings fall right in line. They back us up all the way" (*Shame and Grace*, p. 38).

Lies crumble when they stand alongside the truth. God has already told us that we are forgiven and free forever from condemnation (Rom 8:1,2); that all things are working together for good (Rom 8:28); that we cannot be separated from God's love (Rom 8:35–39); and that God will finish what he has started in us (Phil 1:6). We are not worthless, inadequate, helpless, or hopeless, since Scripture makes it clear that we are God's temple (I Cor 3:16); that we are God's coworkers in the kingdom (2 Cor 5:17–21); that we may approach God with freedom and confidence (Eph 3:12); and that "I can do all things through him who gives me strength" (Phil 4:13).

That's grace. Do we deserve it? Absolutely not. There's a Grand Canyon of separation between deserving something and being worthy of something. It has already been demonstrated that I don't deserve a professional sports career. I don't deserve a Pulitzer Prize. If I did deserve those things, it would be because I had *done* something to earn them. Smedes reminds us that worthiness is different. I am worthy of something not because I have *done* something, but because I *am* somebody of incredible value (*Shame and Grace*, p. 121).

Grace doesn't say, "Look, you're being too hard on yourself. You've got secret assets that you haven't yet figured into your personal inventory." God, with his eyes wide open, accepts his children no matter what loveliness or blasphemy, virtue or vice, resides within our hearts. We are utterly loved simply because God loves us utterly.

Grace doesn't make our lives problem-free, but it does take away one of our most pressing problems. *Grace removes our anxiety about whether God will suddenly change his mind about who we are.* Every day we can know who we are. We are deeply loved servants and disciples of Jesus Christ.

There Is Hope for Us Yet

An Indianapolis Colt I shall never be. But that hasn't kept me off the gridiron. My extended family has established a Thanksgiving Day tradition. Somewhere between the turkey and the pumpkin pie we play a rowdy game of touch football in the front yard. There I was on a recent Thanksgiving, lined up against my in-laws and my own kids. It was all supposed to be simple and fun. And it was—for everybody but me. I don't want to say that I become competitive in any kind of sporting endeavor, but there was no way I was going to let my eight-year-old niece catch a pass on my side of the field. Afterwards Mary Sue shook her head and said, "I can't believe the things you were saying and doing out there." I really didn't know what she was talking about.

Unfortunately it was all recorded on video. Later I sat down to watch the game. I couldn't believe how many opportunities arrived on the film where I could have been a good sport, where I could have smiled, where I could have passed along a simple word of encouragement. Instead, I always seemed to be yelling. "The pine tree is out of bounds!" "Hey, that wasn't a legal catch!" As I watched the video I found myself rooting for myself to become a better person. "Come on," I kept thinking, "grow up! The outcome of this game doesn't matter. These *people* are what matters." When the tape ended I wondered if there was any hope for me.

There *is* hope for me. And there's hope for you. There is hope for anyone who is alive on the outside but dead on the inside. Through the grace of Christ we can be reborn into an entirely new identity. God will never give up on us. We are deeply loved servants and disciples of the King.

Questions for Further Exploration

Personal, one-on-one, or small groups

1. What baggage do you personally bring to the word disciple? If this word has been used in your congregation, what has it meant?

2. What is your opinion of the level of servanthood in Western churches? Where have you seen servants in action, and where is the need the greatest?

3. What vocations and roles receive the greatest honor in your community? What roles tend to be at the bottom of the list?

4. In your own experience, when have you felt not-good-enough in the eyes of God or the eyes of others? How have you addressed this issue?

5. Have you ever had an experience of "institutionalized shame"? How has a church made its own members feel less than whole in the eyes of God? If this is a current issue, what steps can be taken toward wholeness?

Getting Started

On Your Own

Putting our own names into Scripture is a powerful way of claiming God's promises and understanding the identity that God graciously gives to us. Devotionally read aloud a favorite text, inserting your own name. For example, "O Lord, you have searched Bill, and you know Bill; you are acquainted with all of Bill's ways" (Ps 139). Suggested texts might include Psalm 23, Romans 8, Ephesians 1, and I John 3–4.

As a Congregation

To whom is honor accorded in your congregation? Devise a plan to raise the visibility of servanthood. Extend personal words of thanks—face-to-face, written, or both—to every disciple who is involved in some kind of servant role. Establish a year-round ministry that exists solely for the purpose of saying "thank you" to those whose service is all too often out of sight and therefore out of mind.

WHO IS YOUR BARNABAS?

The choice of many basketball fans for coach of all time is John Wooden, who steered the UCLA Bruins to an unprecedented ten national championships from the early 1960s through the early 1970s.

Coach Wooden was born three years before the opening salvo of World War I. His temperament and style seem utterly out of step with today's flamboyant coaches and players. He never lost his cool on the sidelines. He would never allow his players to dunk the basketball, dribble between their legs, or show disrespect for their opponents.

As Wooden revealed to *Sports Illustrated* writer Rick Reilly, he has shaped his life around a few simple commitments. On the twenty-first day of every month he writes a love letter to his wife, Nellie. He tells her how much he misses her, and how he can't wait to see her again. He adds the letter to the stack of other letters that he has written every month since Nellie died in 1985. As a deliberate way of keeping alive his love and respect for her, Coach Wooden has never slept on her side of the bed.

The same kind of discipline characterized his coaching at UCLA. The first half hour of the first practice every year was committed to teaching his players how to put on a sock the right way. "Wrinkles can lead to blisters," he would say. The new players would inevitably sneak looks at each other, rolling their eyes. Here they had come to the biggest of the big-time college basketball programs to strut their stuff, and this old man was teaching them about socks. Finally they would get it right. "Good," he'd say. "Now let's work on the other foot."

Coach Wooden forbade his players to grow facial hair. One day All-American center Bill Walton, the seven-foot-tall most coveted player in the nation, showed up with a full beard. "It's my right," he announced. Wooden asked if he really believed that. Walton said he did. "That's good, Bill," Coach said. "I admire people who have strong beliefs and stick by them, I really do. We're going to miss you." Before day's end Walton had shaved off his beard. That was more than three decades ago. Walton still telephones the coach once a week to tell him that he loves him (Rick Reilly, "The Back Page," *Sports Illustrated*, March 20, 2000).

Those players came to understand that doing the right things the right way would make all the difference in the world. It's called mastering the basics. First we learn how to put on our socks. Then we learn how to put on our shoes. Only then do we learn how to run, to dribble, to pass, and to score.

The greatest college *football* coach of all time may well have been Bud Wilkinson, who led the Oklahoma Sooners to forty-seven consecutive victories, a total that will almost certainly never be surpassed. When asked about his principles of coaching, Wilkinson itemized just three: (1) Tell them what they need to know; (2) Tell them what you told them; (3) Tell them a thousand more times. The drumbeats of a repeated core message bring about success.

History has demonstrated that Wooden and Wilkinson achieved something far beyond their job descriptions. They didn't just teach sports skills. They taught a whole way of life. They continue to be teachers to this day, even to a generation of disciples who were never privileged to meet them.

I Am Somebody's Disciple

In his book *The Divine Conspiracy* Dallas Willard points out that all of us learn how to live—for better or worse—from those who teach us. Each of us is somebody's disciple. "There are no exceptions to this rule, for human beings are just the kind of creatures that have to learn and keep learning from others how to live" (HarperSan-Francisco, 1998, p. 271). Most of us have been discipled, consciously or unconsciously, by a diverse collection of "somebodies" over the years.

For example, I know that it was my parents who taught me that being honest is more important than coming in first. My dad also taught me that money is so scarce that I should almost never spend it or give it away, and that buying dessert at a restaurant is an option reserved for the insane. My piano teacher taught me that when you merely pretend to practice you might fool your mom or your dad, and maybe even yourself, but you can't fool your piano teacher. My scoutmaster taught me how to start a campfire with one match, how to keep the inside of your tent dry in a rainstorm, and how to pluck a chicken—skills I don't use all that much anymore.

My middle school friends taught me that a few well chosen words or a nasty, anonymous note are able to make almost anybody break down and cry. My college professors taught me that God couldn't be trusted. My wife taught me that God could be trusted more than anyone. My children taught me that investing in relationships is more important than attending church committee meetings, and that buying dessert at a restaurant is one of the coolest things anybody can ever do.

All those somebodies have had a role in teaching me how to live. Not every lesson is one that I prize. In fact, one of life's transforming moments is the instant that we realize that we have the power to evaluate what we have learned—to pick through the folk wisdom and truisms and prejudices and principles that make up our rules for existing in this universe—and to ask ourselves if it might not be time to learn from a new teacher, to place ourselves deliberately at the feet of a new master.

That's why it's wonderful to hear Jesus' invitation to follow him. That invitation means that we aren't helplessly imprisoned by who we have already become. We can start life over again. Becoming his disciples means we can relearn how to live from the Son of God himself, so that our thoughts, words, actions, and motives might gradually become more like his.

The Son of Encouragement

How does this learning take place? God sends special teachers into our lives—men and women who by one means or another are called to demonstrate, proclaim, interpret, and model the various essentials of the disciple life. To climb a few feet higher on the spiritual slope we need to receive the encouragement and the extended hands of those who are at least a few feet ahead of us.

"Solo flight" is not a value celebrated in the Bible. Spirituality is imparted and received through relationships. Joshua's leadership lessons arrived via his association with Moses. Ruth looked to her mother-in-law Naomi. Elisha became the protégé of Elijah. Mary found "problem pregnancy" encouragement and partnership in the company of her older relative Elizabeth. Many of the second generation of Christian missionaries, including Titus, Epaphras, and Tychicus, looked to Paul. Apollos received mentoring from Priscilla and Aquila.

It's widely known that "mentor" entered our vocabulary through Homer's mythological epic *Odyssey*. Before his embarkation to the Trojan War, Ulysses placed his son Telemachus in the care of a wise old man, Mentor by name. Homer reveals that Telemachus' education went far beyond book learning. Mentor also gave the lad a healthy dose of street smarts so that years later the son was ready to stand beside the father in the epic final battle for their own family.

The word "Barnabas" might just as easily have emerged as our everyday word for personal teacher. Barnabas was also a citizen of the ancient Mediterranean world but he was no myth. His name first appears during the formative days of the early church in Jerusalem: "Joseph, a Levite from Cyprus, whom the apostles called Barnabas (which means Son of Encouragement), sold a field he owned and brought the money and put it at the apostles' feet" (Acts 4:36–37). Words of unqualified praise are rare in Scripture, but Barnabas is later described as "a good man, full of the Holy Spirit and faith" (Acts 11:24).

It's worth noting that the nickname Barnabas actually means "son of prophecy," but his reputation for raising the level of other people's enthusiasm led Luke to interpret it otherwise. Thus he became the Son of Encouragement.

A Mentor in Action

Nowhere is that more evident than in his relationship with Paul. Having himself been called to the prestigious responsibility of helping oversee the new Gentile converts in Antioch, Barnabas decided to recruit a partner. He remembered the beleaguered Saul of Tarsus. Saul/Paul had never endeared himself to the Christian community, even after his dramatic conversion. Three years after Paul's Damascus experience, it was the generous-hearted Barnabas who had taken a risk and became Paul's sponsor (Acts 9:27). He "went to Tarsus to look for Saul, and when he found him, he brought him to Antioch. So for a whole year Barnabas and Saul met with the church and taught great numbers of people" (Acts 11:25–26). On at least one occasion the pair traveled together to Jerusalem as church emissaries. The upshot is that the credibility attached to Barnabas became attached to Paul, opening the doors for Paul's theological and missional leadership to become central for the whole Church.

Bible scholars suggest that there is something to be learned from the progression of Luke's name ordering for these two men. Sequences are rarely arbitrary.

At the beginning of their first missionary journey, it's "Barnabas and Saul" (Acts 13:7). By the end of the trip, however, Paul has apparently assumed the mantle of leadership from his mentor, as seen in "Saul and Barnabas" (13:43,46,50). The adoring pagans of Lystra, however, trying to pin down the apparent mythological identities of the pair, decide that Barnabas must be Zeus, the king of the gods, while the chatty Paul must be his trusty sidekick Hermes, the messenger of Olympus (14:12). The church in Antioch increasingly saw Paul as the leader ("Paul and Barnabas" in 15:2) while the church in Jerusalem never doubted the seniority of the man they had known much longer ("Barnabas and Paul" in 15:12, 25).

When it came time to launch a second missionary journey, Barnabas exhibited his customary gracious disposition. Despite the fact that his cousin Mark had prematurely opted out halfway through the first trip, Barnabas extended his forgiveness and his hand. Paul, apparently acting out of principle or practicality or both, could not abide Mark's presence. A "sharp contention" arose between them—evidence that even the "founding brothers" of the first century Church occasionally struggled to see things from the same perspective. Paul and Barnabas chose to go separate ways, but Paul's evident respect for his mentor can still be found in his later writings (*Note* I Cor 9:6).

What is the legacy of this relationship? Paul needed a mentor, and God provided one. Barnabas' disposition to see the spiritual potential in others brought Paul from the perimeter to the center—and there is no evidence that Barnabas was ever unhappy that one of the outcomes was his stepping away from the spotlight into Paul's shadow. As the story is reported in the book of Acts, Barnabas became one of God's primary means to release Saul of Tarsus upon the world.

A Continuing Call

This creative and empowering relationship was not intended to be the exception. Discipling is God's norm. Jesus gave himself fully to a dozen men. He lived with them. He loved them. He told them stories and stretched their imaginations. He scolded them when their hearts were calloused. He invited them to walk with him into situations that ranged from the ambiguous to the controversial to the outright dangerous. Sometimes Jesus was formal ("Truly I say unto you..."). Sometimes he was rhetorical ("What's the use of getting the whole world but losing your soul as part of the deal?"). Frequently he engineered opportunities for his disciples to trust God ("Go find something for these 5,000 people to eat..."). On one occasion the Twelve asked for specific training: "Lord, teach us to pray." On every occasion Jesus was communicating, "Let me show you how to live."

It is the absence of this Barnabas role—especially when it is intentionally offered and joyfully received—that impoverishes the contemporary Church's experience of discipleship. When it comes to passing the treasure of God's grace from one generation to another, seminaries have tended to train a few women and men to "stand and deliver." What is everybody else supposed to do? Take notes. Experience has demonstrated that mentoring as many as twelve disciples simultaneously is indeed a full-time calling. It's obvious then that only in a house church could the designated pastor genuinely succeed in bearing the full burden of spiritual mentoring. Almost without exception, North American churches are in need of dozens of individuals who will need to hear and accept the call to become Sons and Daughters of Encouragement.

Is there a Barnabas in your life? If spiritual realities and spiritual understanding are mediated from one person to another, from whom are you learning how to love God and love people?

This is not to say that a single individual should (or even could) fulfill the entire mission of helping another person grow in Christ. Most Christians are discipled by a diverse collection of "somebodies" who are made available by the Spirit at various crossroads in life.

Watching, Helping, Doing

Sometimes our learning has a formal feel to it. One of the challenging tasks of pastoral work is making hospital calls. Hospitals can be forbidding places. People who have checked themselves into hospital rooms are generally not at their best. It can be uncomfortable to walk in on someone who is struggling both physically and emotionally. When I was twenty-five years old I didn't know how to bring encouragement to hospitalized individuals.

I was blessed to have a mentor, however. He was the head of the pastoral staff of the church I was serving. His name is Howard Lindquist. Howard knows how to turn hospital visits into moments of grace. I had been out of seminary for two months when Howard said, "Why don't you take a ride with me this afternoon? Let's go make some hospital visits together."

Howard showed me how to walk into a room. He modeled how to pray for a seriously ill person. He pointed out the best parking spots at the Indianapolis area hospitals—and this is not trivial information—and showed me the side doors and back doors that ultimately would save me who knows how many steps over the next quarter century. Even though I had once taken class notes on hospital visitation, I never needed to reference them again. Howard let me walk beside him one afternoon. He showed me how to care.

There's a well-worn pattern to mentoring that can be expressed in the following sequence of statements:

- I do and you watch.
- I do and you help.
- You do and I help.
- You do and I watch.
- You and I both repeat this pattern with someone else.

Frequently there is no discernible pattern, or even intention, in the passing on of life's lessons. Sometimes a "teachable moment" is formed by a pat on the back, a nod, a frown, or an aptly chosen phrase that will never be forgotten. This is especially true within family relationships.

Someone to Watch over Me

There is a trio of reasons why we each need at least one Barnabas in our life—a straight-talking, encouraging, you'll-hear-the-truth-from-me spiritual friend. First, *we need someone to whom we are accountable*. Left to ourselves, our spiritual plans will go off track. "The spirit is willing but the flesh is weak," Jesus said (Mk 14:38). One of God's provisions for our forward momentum is the presence of a committed advocate.

During the summer of 1999, when the U.S. women's soccer team emerged from global obscurity to win the World Cup, millions of young American females decided they wanted to be just like star forward Mia Hamm. In truth, a great many grown men would have settled for a tenth of the athleticism of Mia Hamm. Girls everywhere began practicing scissor kicks and wearing Number Nine on their jerseys.

Everyone who has ever dreamed the dream of being Mia Hamm, however, has had to face up to an important aspect of reality. None of us can step into her cleats and start kicking goals—we can't perform the way she performs—*unless we choose to live the way she lives*. Mia Hamm has intentionally organized her life around the single goal of becoming a soccer champion. That has necessitated a disciplined approach to what she does and does not eat; hours spent on the practice field; a constant cultivation of teamwork; and myriad non-soccer activities to which she has had to say "No" for many, many years.

Many of us would like to walk triumphantly with Christ. We would revel to hear a clear word of guidance from the Holy Spirit. The problem is that, unless we have consistently committed ourselves to God's priorities as a lifestyle, we're not likely to be "all ears" when God is speaking. Disciples are those who intentionally arrange their lives around the single goal of being transformed into the likeness of Jesus. That requires having a plan and sticking with it. As Dallas Willard puts it, spiritual trying and spiritual training bring about vastly different outcomes (*The Spirit of the Disciplines*, HarperSanFrancisco, 1988, p. 258f). Accountability to a Barnabas is a key way to discern our way forward—and to stay on track.

Someone to Rekindle My Fire

Second, *mentors raise the level of our energy to do God's will*. I was several years into ministry before I realized that personal energy is a renewable resource. Many of us regularly drive ourselves into energy deficits, however, because we fail to understand how draining certain human relationships can be and overlook the unique relationships that are best positioned to renew our spirits.

In an article in the Fall 1984 issue of *Leadership*, entitled "Anatomy of a Spiritual Leader," pastor and author Gordon MacDonald concluded that there are five kinds of people who affect the level of his energy for God. It should be noted that no human being is objectively "stuck" in a particular category—in other words, the same person whose conversation tends to weary your soul may be a neverending source of inspiration for me. MacDonald arbitrarily assigned energy ratings to each of the five groups:

Very Resourceful People. A VRP is a Barnabas, someone who almost always rekindles my vision and re-ignites my enthusiasm for ministry. Energy level (+3).

Very Important People. A VIP is a partner in ministry, someone who shares my passion for a particular work of God. VIP's abound in my own version of Antioch. Energy level (+2).

Very Trainable People. Timothy is the prototypical VTP, the one who looks to me as a Barnabas for spiritual encouragement and discipling. Energy level (+1).

Vice Nice People. Every pastor can testify that a substantial portion of his or her flock is nothing more and nothing less than "nice"—at least when relating to the pastor. VNP's are compliant, don't-rock-the-boat citizens who stand in line to say, "That was a very thoughtful sermon today," but rarely if ever seem to respond to God's call to take up one's cross and go change the world. Energy level (0).

Very Draining People. VDP's can simultaneously be the mission, the obsession, and the bane of church leaders. Draining people have a way of exhausting and discouraging us. In the words of Garth from Wayne's World, "You're sucking my will to live!" Our call is not to "cure" draining people, nor to run from them, as if such things were possible. God's call is that we love difficult people. Energy level (-1).

MacDonald noticed that his own tendency in ministry was to focus on the two categories of people who had the least positive impact on his energy. Like most pastors, he felt that motivating the nice people and "successfully ministering" to the draining people was a strategy that would please God. He spent far less time with mentors, ministry partners, and spiritual apprentices. Upon further reflection he realized that this formula was total depletion. Today he recommends trying to achieve a balance with regard to time investments in each of the five relational areas (Vol. V, No. 4, Fall 1984, p. 106).

If these observations are valid, ignoring a potential Barnabas puts us in peril. Servanthood is often depleting. Many relationships "draw down" our energy and enthusiasm to stay in the fight. Failure to cultivate those few very resourceful people—men and women who almost always "light our fire" and encourage our hearts—will ultimately compromise our ability to minister in Jesus' name.

Someone to Pay Attention to God's Presence

Third, *a spiritual director is a healthy option for many disciples.* Not every Barnabas needs to assume this role, and not every Christian needs to pursue spiritual direction. Nevertheless there is great power in allowing another human being to notice God's workings in the seemingly smallest and most obscure corners of my life. In his book *Working the Angles*, Eugene Peterson suggests these boundaries:

> *Spiritual direction takes place when two people agree to give their full attention to what God is doing in one (or both) of their lives and seek to respond in faith. More often than not*

*... these convergent and devout attentions are brief and un-
planned; at other times they are planned and structured conversations. Whether planned or unplanned, three convictions
underpin these meetings: (1) God is always doing something:
an active grace is shaping this life into a mature salvation;
(2) responding to God is not sheer guesswork: the Christian
community has acquired wisdom through the centuries that
provides guidance; (3) each soul is unique: no wisdom can
simply be applied without discerning the particulars of this
life, this situation.*

(Eerdmans, 1987, p. 150)

Finding Your Barnabas

In summary, spiritual mentors are rare and beautiful people. They
are not easy to find. They are not available at the touch of a button
in on-line chat rooms. There is an unmistakable degree of mystery
in how we find them or how they find us. Why is it that my heart
for God beats so much faster in the presence of certain teachers,
while other individuals—just as committed and earnest—have little
effect on my inner life?

Sometimes we make the happy discovery that Barnabas has
been in front of us all along, and we didn't even discern it. Many
children identify a mom or a dad as the most resourceful person
in their life—for fifty years or more. Barnabas doesn't have to be
nearby (in space or time) to encourage us. Some of us are reener-
gized whenever we access our memories of the first teacher who
really challenged us; the coach who unfailingly modeled integrity;
the drill sergeant who forced us to rethink our motivation; the camp
counselor who taught us to pray; the friend who stood beside us
during the darkest hours of a marital breakup.

Some of the most stirring and original Christian voices of the
past 2,000 years can still be heard through paper and ink. A new
generation of disciples has discovered the wisdom of the Desert
Fathers. Protestants are being mentored by Catholic and Orthodox

contemplatives of previous centuries. The sheer brilliance of John Calvin and C.S. Lewis; the inner zeal of Teresa of Avila; the wit of G.K. Chesterton; the unrelenting passion of Hudson Taylor; the homiletical vigor of C.T. Studd; the soul-expanding story-telling of Fyodor Dostoevsky; the laser focus of Jim Elliott—every one of these holy fires is still burning in a library near you.

Who is your Barnabas? Your answer to that question says more than anything else about your intention to become like Jesus. May God grace you with his lavish gift of a Son or Daughter of Encouragement.

Questions for Further Exploration

Personal, one-on-one, or small groups
1. Who, more than anyone else, taught you how to live? What lessons are you still benefiting from today?

2. What teacher has had the greatest influence on your life? What coach? What pastor?

3. What is the most meaningful and memorable compliment that you have ever received?

4. Can you identify someone in your life from each of Gordon MacDonald's five kinds of people? Would you say that your relationships are balanced in this regard?

5. Have you ever had a spiritual director? How did you meet this person? What is the legacy of their influence on your life?

Getting Started

On Your Own

Do a personal accounting of the mentors in your life. What individuals have shaped your life with God in the past and/or are doing so in the present? Prayerfully discern your current need to be called to a higher level of discipleship. Ask God to provide a Barnabas who can address this need. Make an appointment to sit down with a current mentor to express your hopes in this area, or enlist the support of others (a pastor, small group leader, or friends) to help identify a potential mentor you can approach.

As a Congregation

Just as mentors bless individuals, mentor churches can be powerful assets for other congregations. From what churches has your congregation learned in recent years? Has this been formal, informal, or leader-to-leader? Contemplate the wisdom of moving into a three- to five-year learning relationship with either a national teaching church (which can provide vision, seminars, and resources) or a local church (which can provide friendship and on-site consulting).

Why not both?

WHO IS YOUR TIMOTHY?

The church is the only organization that exists for its nonmembers.
That's a great slogan. Just be careful when you run it past your current members.

A few years ago I was invited to make a presentation to the leadership core of a church that was poised to become more outward-focused. We looked together at Jesus' story about the two sons. That Luke 15 parable is one of the most familiar accounts in the Bible. The younger son brazenly disrespects his father, blows a major chunk of the family's net worth, then staggers home with the faint hope that he can at least sleep outside with the golden retriever. He is stunned—along with everyone else—at the boundless grace of his father, who receives him with open arms and announces, "Let the party begin!"

Only one person cannot give himself permission to have a good time at the party. The older son is furious. His sense of justice has been violated. How can this sorry excuse for a kid brother so disgrace himself and the rest of the family, and then not even have to *pay* for his selfishness? Worse yet, big brother breaks ranks with his father. He seethes, "This son of *yours*..." (meaning, don't you dare put me in the same family photo with this ingrate), while the father reverses the pronoun, searching for a hint of grace in his older son, "This brother of *yours*..."

I was on the verge of pointing out that Jesus clearly intended "religious people" to see themselves in the character of the older son, and then to join God in taking the initiative to reach "sinners." Suddenly one of the lay leaders of that congregation blurted out, "But what about *us*?!" His face was red and the veins on his neck were protruding. "Why are we supposed to care about that one sheep who's out there somewhere when there are already ninety-nine sheep right here, right now, who need to be cared for?" It wasn't a question. It was a projectile. Later I learned that he had lost his job earlier in the week. He found it impossible to think about reaching a hurting world when there was so much hurt on his own plate.

Churches have by and large followed suit. "We want to reach people for Christ...but first we need to stabilize our budget." "What's the point of going after unchurched teenagers when there are 'missing in action' kids in our own congregation? Activating them should be our first priority." "More people? Right. And where are we supposed to put them?" Apart from an unrelenting commitment to an outward focus, churches inevitably are caught in the deadly undertow of the ABCs—attendance, building, and cash—and will find 100 years of reasons not to establish a strategy to make disciples.

Famous Last Words

To be or not to be a blessing for those beyond our own circle: *That is the question*. God's good news is good news indeed when it is on its way through us to the next generation of lifelong learners. The presence of a Timothy—someone who is receiving from us the gifts and insights that we have received from God—is the surest evidence that we actually believe the "famous last words" that Jesus spoke at the end of his ministry on earth.

Christ's Great Commission—his marching orders for every generation, found in various forms at the end of each gospel and at the beginning of Acts (but perhaps most widely cited in Mt 28:19,20)—declares the reason for our existence. Our call is to be disciples who make disciples. Ordinary people, empowered by an extraordinary God, are to go "to every nation." This is the direct fulfillment and the logical extension of the promises that God first gave to Abram (a.k.a. Abraham) in Genesis 12:1–3. It can be argued, in fact, that the rest of the Bible is simply a lengthy commentary on these three verses.

Abraham is told that his descendants will become a great nation, that they will inherit a specific piece of geography (one still very much in dispute), and that he himself will be blessed. God's people may expect to receive God's blessing, which may be defined as the assurance that God has already acted and will continue to act to meet our deepest needs. Being blessed means that God has taken personal responsibility for our well-being. Abraham didn't always *feel* blessed by God. On many days he felt as if his world was collapsing. But God promised to bless this one man and his family, and God kept that promise.

That's not, however, the whole story. As a result of God's graciousness to Abraham this senior citizen "will be a blessing," and "all peoples on earth will be blessed" through him. God blesses people for a reason. We don't merely receive good things from God. We become conduits of these good gifts so that they might be in transit *through* us to other people—even people "at the ends of the earth."

Blessed to Be a Blessing

In contemporary terms, Abraham was not to be an "end user." He was not to be a spiritual cul-de-sac, accumulating God's best stuff and holding on to it for his own purposes. The Bible's formula—first stated in Genesis and echoed throughout both testaments—is this:

(A) We are blessed

(B) To be a blessing.

How do people respond to this call? We can roughly divide the world into four camps.

First, there is the response of the *Cynic*. According to the cynical person neither A nor B in the Bible's "blessing formula" can be trusted. There is no blessing because there is no God—or at least a God about whom we can make any finally definitive statements. Therefore attempting to bless others is a monumental waste of time. Other people need to come up with their own answers and make their own decisions.

The Cynic would say that I am in charge of my own life. I am my own personal project. My chief preoccupation is not with passing along a set of timeless values and behaviors to some teachable Timothy. My real call is to develop myself. As Os Guinness observes in his book, *Time for Truth*, in a postmodern world that is characterized by mobile, fleeting, and superficial contacts, I am in the business of "impression management." How am I coming across right now? Character is a moment-by-moment concern (Baker, 2000, p. 45). Dismissing the reality of both a blessing and a divine Blesser erases any meaningful vision for discipling the next generation.

The second response is that of the *Idealist*. Idealistic people believe that statement B—being a blessing to other people—stands alone. Regardless of whether I am blessed, my goal is to change the world. The world clearly needs to be changed. Bulldozers, bank accounts, and ballistic missiles rule the day. Change will require rhetoric, legislation, revolution, or all of the above.

But whether these efforts are secular or religious, history has demonstrated that such "transformations" are often disastrous. They easily become manipulative. Every one of the great revolutions of the past century was sold as an attempt to bless people. In the end, entire populations were sold out. When statement (A) is left out of the equation—when we attempt to serve others from spiritual emptiness instead of spiritual fullness—we ultimately do damage to others and to ourselves.

Beyond Self-Maintenance

Option number three has a familiar feel. It represents the position of the *Average Churchgoer*. Statement A stands by itself. We are here to enjoy the blessings of God. Period.

Churches typically get the first part of the Bible's formula right. But we fail to cultivate a large enough vision for the second part. To follow the sequence of the six questions posed by this book, it is crucial to know that Christ is Lord. It is liberating to discover that we are his deeply loved servants and disciples. It is transforming to be mentored by a Barnabas. But…if that marks the limits of our experience, then we are living out a mutated version of the Christian faith that has become *all about us*. We may be certain that we are seriously out of step with the Father who extends his arms to the lost son.

I once heard author and evangelist Tony Campolo present the picture of a factory, humming along busily with an immense force of workers, everybody doing his job. A visitor who tours the factory is greatly impressed. At the end of the tour, however, the visitor says, "Wait a minute. You never showed me the shipping department." "What shipping department?" asks the guide. "You know, the place where you send out everything the factory produces." "Oh, we don't have a shipping department. The amazing thing about this factory is that it is entirely self-sustaining. Everything we produce is used to keep the factory running."

How dare we grow churches with a vision no larger than self-maintenance? *Christ's body doesn't exist in order to stay in shape; Christ's body exists to grow.*

Only option four is faithful to the biblical narrative: Our experience of A—being blessed by God—should lead us to the fullest possible expression of B—offering our lives as a blessing for other people. It's safe to conclude that no more than 10–15 percent of American Christians have made the jump from an inward spiritual focus to an outward discipling focus. We are all blessed...but for what purpose?

My own experience is that Christians fear the consequences of focusing on statement B. They worry that in trying to bless others they will somehow lose their own blessing. "I'm just beginning to understand the Bible. Give me a few more years and I'll be ready to help somebody else...but not before." God's good news is that an outward focus doesn't diminish our growth. It accelerates it. Obeying God never shrinks our life with God. It multiplies it.

We're Going to Need a Plan

If disciples aren't super-Christians, then disciple-makers aren't superheroes. Jesus assumed that it would be the normal business of every one of his followers to pass the baton of spiritual life to others. He has fully resourced this project for us. "All authority in heaven and earth has been given to me" (Mt 28:18) "and surely I am with you always, to the very end of the age (28:20). We want for nothing. Grammarians point out that the central verb in the Great Commission is "make disciples." It is modified by three participles: "going" (which could be rendered, "As you go..."), "baptizing" and "teaching." It is as we go through the paces of daily life that we bring, equip, and send out new disciples into the kingdom.

Sitting in church, it's easy to forget that our planning and praying should essentially be about our *next* 100 members—not the 100 members who are already in the fold. One Sunday morning our worshippers discovered that we had torn out the pages of a local phone book—one that serves a metro area of more than a million people. Each bulletin was stuffed with a single page of residential phone numbers.

"God cares about every one of these people," I said. "These are the human beings for whom our church exists." One of our church members began blinking back tears as she stared at the page she had received arbitrarily. It included the phone number of a former teacher she had not seen for years, but whose name had been weighing on her heart for many weeks. In every case, those who aren't yet worshipping and ministering alongside us aren't "just names." They are unique men and women for whom Christ died. How shall we reach them? We're going to need a plan.

Zach Hample is a man with a plan—to catch baseballs. As Rick Reilly learned in an interview with him for *Sports Illustrated*, Hample was still a 23-year-old student from New York City when he wrote *How to Snag Major League Baseballs*. Over the previous eleven years he had personally brought home 1,680 major league balls. At the time of publication he had a streak of 264 games in which he had caught at least one. What's most amazing is that Zach averages six balls a game—that's six times in a span of just a few hours what most of us would consider a once-in-a-lifetime event.

How does Zach do it? As he explains in his book, "Use your head." Be in the right place at the right time. Zach knows when every major league ballpark opens for batting practice, so he's always first in line to catch a batting practice foul ball. Zach has memorized where certain hitters are likely to foul off pitches. If you want to catch a real baseball, whom should you sit next to? Zach suggests, "Look for a family fascinated by the JumboTron, or very old people" (April 9, 2001, p. 100).

If only the average congregation devoted half as much energy and research to making disciples as Zach Hample devotes to snagging baseballs.

We're going to need a plan.

This is not the same thing as searching for a program or a package, that elusive spiritual "magic bullet" that will eliminate all our need to pray, to discern God's will, and to trust the work of the Spirit. We cannot do an end run around our fundamental need to place ourselves, humbly and helplessly, at God's disposal. What if we have planned the next six months of ministry in such a way that God doesn't even need to show up for our plans to succeed? Should we then be surprised if we later discern that our tactics and goals weren't even on the Spirit's radar screen?

Christianity One-On-One

Dallas Willard devotes the final chapter of his book *Renovation of the Heart* to various questions surrounding disciplemaking in the local church. He writes, "No special talents, personal skills, educational programs, money or possessions are required to bring this to pass." Amen! Willard continues, "A simple goal for the leaders of a particular group would be to bring all those in attendance to understand clearly what it means to be a disciple of Jesus and to be solidly committed to discipleship in their whole life...We don't want to be picky over the details of how this is done. It just needs to be done" (Navpress, 2002, p. 244).

How is God calling you to reach the next generation for Jesus Christ? How are you going to "get it done" where you already live and work and worship?

Our church has chosen to place personal disciple-making at center stage—to declare that one person helping another person become more like Jesus is an attainable, normal, and desirable activity for every affiliate of our congregation. We are at the beginning stages of what we expect to be at least a 10-year process of changing the culture at ZPC. Through an initiative called TrailBlazers, church members of all ages are given an entire year of training and coaching in the basics of the Christian life. Within the first three months of that year each TrailBlazer participant is asked to find an apprentice—to approach one other person and say, "Would you be willing to meet with me on a regular basis for at least the next twelve months, so that we might learn and grow together in what it means to follow Christ?"

The motto of TrailBlazers is "Christianity one-on-one." Our experience is like that of most churches: One size and one style does not fit all when it comes to helping disciples go forward with Jesus. Some of our members learn best in classroom settings. Others respond well to directed private study. Still others prefer small group settings. It is our conviction that the greatest unexplored opportunity for discipleship in the average church is the one-on-one, Barnabas-to-Paul or Paul-to-Timothy kind of relationship, in which two people agree to target deeper growth in the six marks of a disciple over a long period of time.

One sentence from Paul's hand, more than any other, helps us understand what it means to pass the baton of faith. It's 2 Timothy 2:2: **"And what you have heard from me through many witnesses entrust to faithful people who will be able to teach others as well."** Let's do an anatomy of this verse by asking the question, "What does a discipling relationship look like?"

Discipling Is Relational

Our first observation is simple. Discipling is *relational*. People learn how to better love and follow Jesus in the context of a focused friendship.

The "you" in 2 Timothy 2:2 refers to a spiritual apprentice named Timothy, and the "me" refers to Paul. Paul had recruited Timothy at least fifteen years earlier on his second pass through Timothy's home town of Lystra, in the province of Asia. Since Timothy is still described as "young" at this stage in his life (*see* I Tm 4:12), he must have been a very young person indeed at the beginning of their friendship.

On the pages of the New Testament we have the privilege of watching as Timothy, a raw and sometimes painfully shy recruit, gradually grows up into his role as Paul's apparent successor. He is sincere and devoted but is sometimes intimidated by theological opponents. He suffers at least one ministry setback, in Corinth—trying to corral those belligerent believers turns out to be just a shade easier than herding cats. Paul tenderly describes him as "my true child in the faith" (I Tm 1:2) and "my son" (I Tm 1:18), and even says to the Philippians, "I have no one else like him, who takes a genuine interest in your welfare" (1:20).

Paul makes another statement that confirms he wasn't the first discipling presence in Timothy's life: "I have been reminded of your sincere faith, which first lived in your grandmother Lois and in your mother Eunice and, I am persuaded, now lives in you" (2 Tm 1:5). There were already three generations of faith under Timothy's roof. A number of our TrailBlazers have discovered that the spiritual apprentice of God's choosing is already sitting at their dinner table every evening.

Discipling is Personal

Timothy didn't learn how to follow Jesus by taking a course at a local community college and then memorizing his notes. In 2 Timothy 2:2 Paul refers to "what you have heard *from me....*" The basics of the disciple life are mediated through the unique personality and style of the discipler. Even the few details that we have in hand about the earliest Christian leaders reveal a wide range of temperament and approach.

Stephen was a confronter. Protective gear was nice to have nearby during his preaching: "You stiff-necked people, with uncircumcised hearts and ears!" (Acts 7:51). If you're a pastor and you've ever thought, "You know, I'd love to get a few things off my chest during my last sermon here"—well, that was Stephen's *very* last sermon. Philip preferred a more Socratic approach: "Do you understand what you are reading?" (Acts 8:40). Epaphras let his fervent prayer, his servanthood, and his hard work do the talking (Col 4:12).

The good news is that we do not need to slavishly imitate or reproduce one approach to ministry. During my college years I belonged to a fellowship that had carved out Wednesday evenings for "cold contacts" at the student union on my campus. Week after week I complied with the directive of my group leader and targeted individuals who were eating or studying alone: "Do you have a few minutes to talk about spiritual things?"

Even though God worked through a few of those conversations, the long-term legacy of such "bombing runs" (aside from years of post-traumatic stomach aches on Wednesday evenings) was a strongly negative association with faith-sharing. Whenever I thought of evangelism I automatically felt uncomfortable. I felt like a failure. I felt guilty and angry, too, until I came to understand that God has especially wired me to share my faith through a style of Q & A and give-and-take that naturally happens during long-term relationships.

Discipling Is Theologically Grounded

What kind of heritage is Paul passing to Timothy? Is it a set of novel spiritual musings that he zipped off during a moment of personal inspiration? No, Paul is faithfully delivering what he himself received from "many witnesses" or *marturiois* ("martyrs"). In the first century a martyr denoted a public witness to the truth. The evolution of that word into its present meaning is evidence that Christian truth-telling could be terminally costly.

Theologically we do not reinvent the wheel. Helping others grow in Christ means guiding them along the pathways of previous generations. This would include an experience of all six marks of a disciple—not just the one or two that are the easiest and most natural "fits" with our present character and motivation. Good news always reaches us from someone else—on its way to another some-one—and we are accountable for making sure the whole message arrives.

Paul tells Timothy he needs to entrust these teachings to other people. In Greek the word "entrust" means making a secure run to the bank to deposit a treasure. Here we need to be careful to re-member that discipling another person is not doing a "data dump" into a particularly teachable brain. Paul knew Timothy. He loved him. Disciples are not widgets. Every human being is a uniquely crafted bearer of God's image, and the ways we teach, model, pray, and share life with that person will always include elements of sheer mystery.

Discipling Is Intentional

In *Holy Living* Jeremy Taylor, a seventeenth-century Anglican bishop, wrote that "some friendships are made by nature, some by contract, some by interest, and some by souls" (Mead, Frank S., *12,000 Reli-gious Quotations*, p. 157). Not every discipling relationship begins on purpose. Effective ones, however, are nearly always character-ized over the long run by intentionality. It's plain that Timothy and Paul established (or at least sustained) a spiritual partnership for the express purpose of helping the former learn what the latter had already gleaned from others.

All of us are involved in hundreds of unintentional relationships every week. Most of them are exceedingly brief. Few of them bear

significant potential for personal transformation. A discipling relationship, on the other hand, assumes a purposeful direction and is
nourished by regularity. A covenant of one year is a good place to
start.

If there is a Timothy in your life, there is no rush to "get through
the curriculum." Listening is more important than talking—and
learning how to listen to a particular human being takes a long
time. One of the reasons that relationships are spiritual adventures
is that we can never know precisely how the Spirit will work in the
context of another human life.

Discipling Is Transformational

By God's grace our aim is to help present the "whole counsel of
God" to a whole person. Bob Jordan describes four of the major
arenas in which this transforming interaction can take place.

Study: The publishing world has produced a wide assortment
of material useful for disciple-making relationships. We need to
look for resources that are appropriate to our apprentice's journey
and method of learning. Examples include book and Bible studies,
conferences and retreats, and learning from nature and the world
in general.

Reflection: Knowledge is great, but understanding is even better. Understanding often involves seeing connections, which usually
happens best when we slow down. Practices that have been useful
to many Christians in the past include fasting, silence and solitude,
simplicity, meditation, reflective reading, prayer, and meaningful
conversations.

Action: Experiences can often teach volumes in a relatively short
period of time. Actions not only help form ideas, but test them
and help us grasp them comprehensively—"body, mind, soul, and
strength." Transformation helps take place as we join our Timothy
in worship, meeting the needs of neighbors, short-term mission

trips, team ministries, and working with local missions.

Reception: Transformation ultimately depends on the hand of God. That means it does not always require the activity of the one being changed into Christ's likeness. On many occasions all we need to do is receive. Here we have in mind the sacraments, anointing with oil, the laying on of hands, healing prayer, and our experience of the love of God and others (unpublished work by Bob Jordan, Associate Pastor for Discipleship, Zionsville Presbyterian Church).

Discipling Is Reproducible

Paul commands Timothy to entrust what he has learned to "faithful people" (*pistois*). Where will we find such people? Because of our culture's extraordinary speed of communication and the relative social isolation of many vocations, disciple-making will increasingly be observed within webs of existing relationships. Realtors will help fulfill the Great Commission by reaching other realtors. The same will be true amongst teachers in a particular school district, sales reps along the East coast of the United States, and Internet "gamers" who no longer think it strange to be teamed in cyberspace with Korean, Romanian, and Guatemalan partners.

The decisive phrase in 2 Timothy 2:2 is the last one: *who will be able to teach others also*. Effective disciple-making thus involves four generations. In this verse we see Paul, who's pouring into Timothy, who's doing the same thing with a few others—with the key proviso that Timothy must find a way to carry out this mission so that the chain will not be broken—to ensure that the third generation will raise up a fourth generation. Our disciple-making initiatives must be designed not just to help disciples learn, but to help disciples learn how to *teach* what they have learned. One of the most moving visual images in recent years at ZPC was a group of four women who stood at the pulpit. The first introduced the second as her spiritual apprentice...who then introduced the third…who then told the story of sharing her life with the fourth—all over a period of several years.

As your "Timothy" considers making a commitment to disciple another person, what gifts are you as a discipler able to provide? You will be specially positioned to say, "Do for someone else what I have done for you. I'll help you get started. You can count on my prayers, my coaching, and my support. *You can do this—and the kingdom will be greater because of it.*"

The harvest of seeds planted years earlier in discipling relationships is one of the greatest joys in the Christian experience. Sunday school teachers and youth leaders are often struck with awe as "their kids" grow up, get married, bear children of their own, and navigate all of these passages with faith-molded hearts.

More than a decade after I stepped away from a particular youth leadership position, I ran into Mike, who had always been one of the quieter high schoolers in my flock. As we reminisced about old times I suddenly winced and said, "You know, one of the worst weekends of my life was that February ski trip we took to Michigan when the weather turned sixty degrees! I ended up 'winging' an entire indoor retreat. That was such a flop. I'll never forget how low I felt on the bus ride home." Mike stared at me, incredulous. "Man, you still don't even know, do you? That was the weekend I became a Christian."

God is always at work in spiritually focused friendships—even when we don't have the eyes to see. Have you made a commitment to help bring about Jesus' last and greatest wish for this world? If you don't have a plan, are you willing to learn one? If you don't have the motivation, are you willing to seek it? If you don't have a Timothy, will you begin praying right now about who that might be?

Questions for Further Exploration

Personal, one-on-one, or small groups

1. Does your church have a "shipping department"? What is currently being shipped?

2. Can you name someone who has learned something about following Christ from you? What did they learn?

3. What has been the most transforming friendship of your life? Why?

4. If a church ideally should be organized around the needs of its next 100 members, who do you think your church's next 100 members will need? How will those needs be different from the felt needs of your current members? What will be required to reach those 100 people?

5. Of the four arenas of transformation (study, reflection, action, and reception), which has God used most often in your own life?

Getting Started

On Your Own

Approaching a potential Timothy can feel daunting. Begin with prayer. Ask God to open your eyes to the presence of someone who has been praying to meet someone like you. Be simple and direct: "Would you be willing to spend time with me during the next year? It would be a privilege to share with you some of the things that God has been sharing with me, and we could learn from each other." Few people ever hear such a stunning offer of grace. Be confident that even if the answer is No or Not Yet, God has prepared someone to learn from your life.

As a Congregation

One way to cast a congregational vision for one-on-one discipling is to publicly present several spiritual "generations." Bring together three, four, or five individuals who have sequentially helped each other follow Christ (A discipled B, B discipled C, etc.). This is particularly vivid if one of the disciples is a member of the pastoral staff.

6

WHERE IS YOUR ANTIOCH?

Right now the place where you are sitting may seem absolutely silent. Physicists assure us, however, that it is permeated by sound. All you need is the right receiver to pick up the countless thousands of messages that are zinging past you or moving right through you on radio waves and television waves. You are currently sharing space with soap operas, CNN newscasts, soccer games, reruns of "The Brady Bunch," and commercials for deodorants, long-distance telephone rates, and The Clapper. In your immediate vicinity are Beethoven, Tony Bennett, and Britney Spears, and the Baja Men are singing, "Who Let the Dogs Out?" *Be warned*: Thinking about this longer than two minutes can be depressing.

The good news is that you can decide whether or not to listen in. It's all a matter of tuning. In an analogous way, the Holy Spirit has saturated your reality with communication from God. The invisible world is alive with the king of the universe. Your job is to listen to what the king is saying. But how do we tune in? If God is always speaking to us, as Scripture affirms—and if we can trust God not to be playing a game of cosmic hide-and-seek—how and where will we hear God's voice?

Tuning in to the Spirit

Our hearts become tuned to the frequency of heaven whenever we choose to say, "Lord, I am your servant. Your servant is listening. Speak to me about where you would like me to go and what you would like me to do" (1 Sm 3:10).

Paul asked, "What shall I do, Lord?" during his very first encounter with Christ (Acts 22:10). On that occasion he heard a voice from heaven. God also directed him by means of the trembling hands of Ananias (9:17); the protective intervention of the Jerusalem church (9:29–30); the words of the prophet Agabus (11:27–30); the hard reality of persecution (13:50–51); official appointment by a local church (15:2); unspecified blocking by the Holy Spirit (16:7–8); the vision of a man from Macedonia (16:9–10, about which there will be more in the next chapter); and numerous other means, including dreams, natural disasters, being "caught up to heaven" (2 Cor 12:3–4), and edicts by governing authorities. We should not omit Paul's obvious gift for strategic discernment. God clearly worked through his ability to assess the social, political, and geographical opportunities at hand, and then to make wise choices.

In short, Paul received direction from God through myriad means and circumstances. He didn't keep scheduling trips down the Damascus highway in the mistaken conviction that "this is how God always speaks to me." Apparently God spoke to Paul like that exactly once. We also see evidence that Paul chiefly discerned what God was doing in his life by looking in the rear-view mirror. From time to time he confidently announced plans that he wasn't able to carry out (Rom 15:23–24 and I Cor 16:5–9, for example). Only as he looked back (2 Cor 1:15-2:4, for instance) was he able to see that the Spirit had different objectives for him to fulfill.

One place stands out as a setting where Paul's heart was trained to "tune in" to the voice of God. That place was Antioch. Paul spent years ministering there. He enjoyed the company of a spiritual peer group that cared for him. Antioch was Paul's home base. It served as the launching point for all three of his missionary journeys. Antioch was where Paul's ultimate calling was both discerned and blessed.

Each of us needs an Antioch—one or more settings in which we can be ourselves in the company of a few other faithful people. We will be greatly blessed if we have found at least one place where it is safe to "try on" and "try out" the various visions to which God may be calling us—where we can hear the truth about ourselves without fear; where trusted friends can help calibrate our inner tuners to hear the voice of God; and where those same colleagues are willing and able to bless us on our way.

Not a Special Place, but Special People

Antioch was situated near the Mediterranean Sea, only fifteen miles up the Orontes River. We would not have mistaken it, however, for Club Med. It was a large city—the third biggest in the Empire, after Rome and Alexandria—but its 200,000 residents were squeezed into a walled-in area only one mile by two miles. That represents a population density higher than the modern day slums of Calcutta and Mexico City, and is twice as populous as Manhattan. Sanitation was horrific. Rodents, insects, and thousands of domesticated animals shared the living space. One-third of the children died before their sixth birthday, and 70 percent of the adults were gone by age 26. It's no wonder that the word *necropolis* ("city of death") was a frequent designation for urban areas in the ancient world.

Antioch was famous for its diversions, including chariot racing and the adoration of Daphne. In Greek mythology Daphne was the maiden who was turned into a laurel tree to save her from the amorous intentions of Apollo. In the laurel groves outside town, Daphne worship provided ample opportunities for would-be Apollos to capture local prostitutes. It was in this environment—not exactly crafted for monastic reflection—that Paul and a special group of ministry partners invested years in teaching and listening to God.

Our own "Antioch," in other words, doesn't have to be heaven on earth. We don't need to find a special physical setting. What matters is being present with a few special people who are committed to listening to the Holy Spirit. Paul was blessed with just such a consortium during the formative years of his ministry.

Hearing God Together

How have God's people over the centuries learned about God's ways? The writer of Proverbs 2:4,5 tells us, "If you look for it as silver and search for it as for hidden treasure, then you will understand the fear of the Lord and find the knowledge of God."

That sounds like hard work. Why doesn't God simply provide us with cerebral downloads of spiritual wisdom on an as needed basis? That's how it works in the movie *The Matrix*. You don't know how to fly that helicopter? We can transmit the knowhow to your brain within seconds. How convenient it would be to pray for and receive helpful programs such as "How to Be Patient When the Dryer Breaks," and "Mending Fences With Irascible Neighbors." God created us, however, to grow into Christlikeness and to hear the voice of our Lord within a web of living relationships—with God and with each other. God not only wants to be pursued, he wants to be pursued through our experience of community. *Together* we need to learn how to become like Jesus, and to discern where Jesus is sending us next.

Where is your Antioch? In all likelihood it is not just one place. As a pastor I regularly spend time with the following groups: my own family; my extended family; my neighbors; a local ministers' association; my denominational governing body; my church staff, numerous groups, teams, ministries, and classes within my church; a small group of five couples; the local Rotary Club; a regional chat group of pastors; and a national prayer covenant group. Which of those associations do I call my "spiritual home base"?

The answer is, "It depends." The Spirit does the work of encouragement, correction, assurance, transformation, and guidance in my life through a number of those groups in a number of different ways. It all depends on the circumstances, the issues, and the timing.

A molecular illustration may be helpful. In a molecule different kinds of atoms are bonded to each other. Depending on the atomic components, some of those bonds may be fragile. Others may be almost unbreakable. For example, despite living on the same street for more than a dozen years, my neighborhood relationships remain comparatively weak. My relationship with my five "covenant brothers," however, is intense—even though I see those men for only three days each year. Our goal should not be to collect as many groups as possible, since the majority of those relationships would turn out to be superficial. Instead we should aim to be "in" at least one place where spiritual accountability, truth-telling, and listening to God are priority activities.

Ideally our own experience of family should be a kind of Antioch. Glowing descriptions of Christian marriage and parenting would lead us to believe that much of what we need to hear from God will be mediated at home. That is the ideal. Reality falls far short. The grievous level of family breakups within the American Christian community leads us to this sad observation: Deep disappointments are dominating the agenda of far too many homes. It simply hurts to be in many churchgoing families. There is a greater need than ever for "homes away from home"—small groups for personal support and transformation—where estranged family members can reclaim their love for spouses, parents, and children.

What about the apostle Paul? The details of his family life represent one of those "blind spots" on his biography. Aside from the revelation of his singleness at the time he wrote I Corinthians (*see*

7:7), our information is limited. It's interesting to note that Paul returned to his hometown of Tarsus shortly after his conversion. That's where Barnabas found him (Acts 11:25) in order to bring him to Antioch—the city that became his spiritual home base for the remainder of his adult life.

In Search of True Community

Disappointment is also a common experience for those who search for community at denominational gatherings. "We are all leaders of the Body of Christ. We all profess a love for God. So why are these meetings so boring and predictable? Why isn't there a higher level of rejoicing, unity, and praise? Worse yet—why do we so often get sidetracked by dissension and politicking? It's big church vs. small church, left vs. right, generation vs. generation. *Can't we all just get along?*

M. Scott Peck provides a remarkable set of observations about community in his book *The Different Drum*. True community is rare. It is not an easy thing to achieve. Almost all groups, of all sizes, settle for what Peck calls "pseudo-community." In pseudo-community everybody plays nice. There is politeness and deference and peacekeeping. Nobody rocks the boat. We may even go home and say, "Now, that was a good meeting." But it wasn't true community. (Touchstone Books, 1998, multiple pages).

Authentic unity and partnership with other human beings is characterized by God's gift of peace, or *shalom*. Real community requires peace *making*, not peace *keeping*. There is a pathway to true community. Peck calls it "chaos." Chaos takes place when at least one person confronts an issue that simply has to be faced. He thereby pulls the veil off pseudo-community and reveals the play-acting that has been going on.

Few people enjoy the experience of chaos. Therefore few groups take the risk of real confrontation and dialogue that is necessary to get to true community. Many spouses prefer to keep a lid on their most explosive issues. They settle for a pseudo-community marriage. Coworkers may share the same space forty hours a week for many years without talking about the elephant in the middle of the office. A pastor and board may become fixated on minor issues because it's too threatening to say out loud, "We have a real problem here."

There is no mistaking the fact that Jesus calls his followers to true community. In the Bible there are fifty-eight commands that combine a verbal form with the words "one another" or "each other." Interestingly, they are all in the New Testament. None of them is for cowards: Forgive one another (Col 3:13); admonish one another (Col 3:16); confess your sins to each other (Jas 5:16); love each other "as I have loved you" (Jn 13:34): These are the kinds of courageous behaviors that deliver us from politeness into relational messiness—but bear the promise of reconciliation and understanding.

Most larger Christian gatherings—including worship services, conferences, and denominational meetings—provide brief, almost haunting experiences of community. For a few minutes we let down our masks. We get off our high horses. We suddenly sense that "God is truly in this place, and I did not know it." More often than not, however, the gravity of our pseudo-community instincts drags us back to earth. Where then can we go for a deeper experience of openness and partnership with other disciples?

For more and more churches, the answer is small groups.

The Promise of Small Groups

What do we know about small groups? First, let me offer a disclaimer. My remarks will barely do justice to the ever-expanding body of congregational experience and research that is underway in this part of the wider Church. I strongly encourage you to read widely, and from a variety of authors. The shape of "small group spirituality" in America is still very much in formation. What we know is that small groups may generally be described as intentional, face-to-face gatherings of from three to fourteen people, which meet at least once each month (preferably two, three, or four times) for the primary purpose of helping their members grow in their quest to become more like Jesus. They can be classified into three geometric shapes: "round" groups that focus on study, shared spiritual life and accountability; "square" groups that center on tasks, mission endeavors, and/or governance; and "triangle" groups that prioritize the experience of shared prayer, healing, and support.

Such mini-communities have always been part of the Christian story. Jesus taught the crowds, partnered in ministry with the Seventy, but discipled and shared life with the Twelve. Healthy small groups can be safe places for disciples to work on the "one another" commands and can provide the intimacy and trust necessary for believers to "speak the truth in love" to each other.

Small groups are also a preferred way of keeping a church from growing colder as it grows larger. By valuing relationships, these groups reflect a greater commitment to people than to tasks. The old paradigm for church life can be summarized, "We get together to get things done, and use people to make it happen." A spiritually vital congregation has to affirm, "We get together to build each other up, and the Kingdom is built as a consequence." Small groups are a primary place for such relationship-building to take place.

For the past decade-and-a-half, a number of church futurists have reckoned that the viable and life-transforming congregation of the twenty-first century will be a church *of* small groups, not merely a church *with* small groups. Meeting regularly with a few other people won't be a side dish on the ecclesiastical menu. Rather, group life will prove to be the single most important way for most people to move forward in discipleship. Some theorists have gone even further. They have bet the house on small groups. Intentional gatherings of about a dozen people will be able to carry the *whole burden* of discipleship. The entirety of the Christian experience—worship, education, fellowship, pastoral care, missions, and evangelism—will be lived out in groups.

Is that vision proving to be a reality? The jury is still out. Our own experience is ambiguous. Although our congregation has enjoyed the blessing of gathering in small groups of many kinds (including round ones, square ones, and triangular ones), we have come to the conclusion that they cannot carry the main burden of discipleship all by themselves. Growing into the full life of Jesus requires levels of learning, doing, and risking that are beyond the experience of the average small group—not *every* small group, but the *average* small group.

So what's to celebrate about small groups? Plenty. They can be exceptional places for assimilation, friendship-building, short-term mission projects, accountability, encountering a Barnabas or a Timothy (or both), and learning how to hear God's voice over extended periods of time. In short, a healthy small group can be a wonderful Antioch.

One Style Does Not Fit All

For several years we actively pursued a standardization of group life at ZPC—trying to make leaders and participants jump through the same behavioral hoops. Today we take a much more participant-defined approach. Some individuals who are drawn to groups appreciate structure; others crave spontaneity. Some participants need to learn Christianity 101; others are ready to wade through deeper waters. Some group members are eager to serve; others are looking to give or to receive intensive care. The Spirit should not be bound by artificial or limited agendas for small groups.

The fact is, small groups are exceedingly useful. They accomplish community to a degree that's simply unattainable when only one shepherd (the pastor) is deployed over the flock. Leaders of smaller congregations sometimes say, "I don't see the relevance or urgency of establishing a small group network. We have only seventy-five people in worship." That presumes that a solo pastor can and should be available to address the many crises and crossroads of spiritual growth that will be typical for seventy-five average human beings.

The larger our church grew, the more I mourned the fact that I became cut off from the daily spiritual warp and woof of most of our members. But I take courage from the fact that during any given week there are numerous groups that are gathering—out of my sight, but never out of God's sight—where authentic confession, confrontation, praying, learning, and encouragement are taking place.

Over the years the one method of starting new groups at ZPC that has worked better than any other has been the identification of a leader or lead couple, who then invite others into a shared experience. New members end up sampling and staying in particular small groups for the same reason people are drawn to particular churches: They are invited by people they already know and trust.

Lay Leadership is the Key

The key currency in a small-group church is lay leadership. How do gifted and called group leaders emerge? In classic chicken-and-egg style, we observe that the best new leaders are those who are graduates of healthy groups—but we won't have healthy groups unless we start with exceptional leaders.

Early on we experimented with a leadership training method that's been called the Johnny Appleseed strategy. Johnny Appleseed was the early American who strolled across the Midwest planting apple orchards. The fruit of his work continued to appear years after he had moved on to the next county. In like fashion, on four occasions I gathered groups of from eight to twelve individuals and pledged to spend up to one year with them in a kind of trial small group. They would learn "on the job" how to lead a small group and then head out to form groups of their own, while I would "seed" the next group of learners. The good news? This was a great way to draw some very gifted people into small group life. The bad news? Even a so-called trial small group doesn't welcome breaking up. Ultimately God has led more than half of those group participants into lay leadership roles.

The truth is that there has never been a single day in which we have enjoyed a surplus of lay leaders. We always seem to be writing a want ad for five more. At times the Spirit dramatically presents us with a few new individuals who are obviously gifted and available to lead. At other times the leadership incubator has a population of zero. We don't lose heart, however, because we know two things: (1) The task of developing new leaders *cannot* be set aside, except at our peril, and (2) *God* is ultimately responsible for calling members of the Body into new expressions of ministry—and God will certainly do so.

The Radically Committed Group

There is one kind of small group that comes closer to Paul's experience at Antioch than any other. It is the cadre of like-minded disciples who intentionally hold each other to a higher standard. They refuse to settle for pseudo-community. They are not in the group for themselves. They are there for each other.

In Acts 13:1–3 Luke tells us, "In the church at Antioch there were prophets and teachers: Barnabas, Simeon called Niger, Lucius of Cyrene, Manaen (who had been brought up with Herod the Tetrarch) and Saul. While they were worshipping the Lord and fasting, the

Holy Spirit said, 'Set apart for me Barnabas and Saul for the work to which I have called them.' So after they had fasted and prayed, they placed their hands on them and sent them off."

Barnabas and Saul we know well. Who were the other three members of the Antiochean leadership team? Simeon is a Jewish name, but Niger is a Latin loanword that means "Black." Scholars speculate that he was from Africa. Not only so, but Simeon may well have been the "Simon of Cyrene" from Luke 23:26 who had been compelled by the Romans to carry Jesus' cross to Golgotha. In that case, he really did have the most interesting testimony in town. Nothing else is known of Lucius of Cyrene. Manean is described as a *syntrophos* or "foster brother" of Herod Antipas, the man who arranged for the beheading of John the Baptist and who interviewed Jesus on the night he was arrested. That meant Manaen had perhaps the *second* most interesting testimony on the block.

The one thing we know of this group is its spiritual synergy. They sought God's voice. God spoke. They responded in faith. They divided their fellowship so the world might be blessed. Along the way they fasted (both before and after the Spirit's communication), worshipped, provided laying on of hands, and then sent the pair on their way (the Greek verb for *sent* has the sense of "releasing them from further obligation").

Antioch is the place where we know we are seeking God's will for our lives. Antioch is that small circle that is willing to do for us so that we might be called and empowered to do for others. Sending is one of the majestic gifts of a true Antioch.

We Cannot Do It Alone

I am privileged to enjoy a few relationships that aim for such mutual, radical commitment. The truth remains, however, that none of us will experience significant life change unless other people are there to help us—challenging us, encouraging us, and sometimes saying, "What in the world were you thinking?" Becoming like Jesus isn't easy. I cannot do it on my own. If I'm not in community with other disciples, I know what will happen. I will cheat. I will speak the words but not live the life. I will fail to hold myself accountable to the ways in which my wandering heart incurably pursues that which is less than God's best. Only an examined life, and a life that is examined by others on the same journey, can ever look like Jesus.

As a young Christian I discovered that I could make a certain amount of spiritual progress just by willing myself to cease a few behaviors, and by adopting a few "religious" ones. It was a heady and exciting time. It didn't last very long.

I got stuck—stuck at the same level of obedience to God (and the same level of disobedience), year after year after year. Getting me unstuck has been the mission of several very important people in my life. They have permission to look into my soul and to comment on what they see. I meet with five other men, who live in various spots around the country, every spring for three days. We have made a covenant to pray for each other every day in between. Another friend, every few weeks without fail, says to me, "Glenn, are you serious about living this life? Are you stepping out of your comfort zone? What are you doing right now that is forcing a deeper reliance on God?"

No price tag can be placed on focused spiritual friendships. In a healthy small group people can challenge each other to "go for it." If you had determined to go bungee jumping, would you go by yourself? Most people who hurl themselves into an abyss secured only by an elastic cord choose to be accompanied by one or two other people who have agreed to share their terror and ecstasy. Going deeper into the disciple life is a certifiable spiritual bungee jump—and it's worth every minute of terror and ecstasy that ensues.

Our Desires and God's Desires

We can make one final observation concerning Antioch. We don't know what Paul, Barnabas, Lucius, Simeon, and Manean had been praying for. There is no evidence that when the Holy Spirit spoke, Paul and Barnabas thought, "Ah, at last. This is what we've been dreaming about." The Spirit's voice may well have been a surprise. Nothing in the text reveals that any of these five men had a clue as to what was going to happen next. All they knew is that a new journey was beginning, and it was time to set out.

When we seek God's voice, our prayers must be open-ended. We don't know what God will say. We don't know how the Spirit will direct. All we know is that God can be trusted, and that he is bigger than our hopes and our fears and our modest understanding of what is happening around us.

Three hundred years after Christ a rebellious, immoral, yet brilliant teenager named Augustine was growing up in North Africa. Augustine drove his godly mother Monica to her knees. She begged Augustine to come to Christ, but he rebuffed her at every turn. Ultimately he determined to skip town and sail toward greater adventures in Italy. Today this would be akin to a teenage boy telling his mother that he's weary of Des Moines and is going to move on to Las Vegas.

Monica spent a sleepless night pleading with God to block his path. "Please let him stay here in Africa so that one day he might find and serve you!" Her prayers went unanswered. Augustine sailed away unhindered, leaving Monica feeling helpless and confused before the sheer silence of God. But God knew best. In Italy, Augustine came under the influence of Ambrose, bishop of Milan, who mentored him into a spiritual life that would bless and transform the history of the Church.

Later in life, Augustine reflected on his mother's sincere prayers that night. He was grateful—grateful that God chose not to answer them. If God had said "yes" to her stated desire, then her real desire for his spiritual awakening might never have been satisfied. Augustine wrote this prayer of thanks: "Thou, in the depth of thy counsels, hearing the main point of her desire, regarded not what she then asked, that thou mightest make me what she ever desired."

When we seek God's direction we won't always hear everything we'd like. But this we can count on: God will be faithful to us. When it is time for a new journey, God will tell us exactly what we need to know.

Is there a place in your life where a few faithful friends are listening with you for that word from God? *If you don't have an Antioch today, are you willing to help form one?*

Questions for Further Exploration

Personal, one-on-one, or small groups

1. Describe a personal experience in which God guided you. How did God use other people to communicate his will for your life?

2. Where is your current Antioch? Do you have more than one? What are the formal and informal places in which you meet with others who are endeavoring to live for God?

3. Describe a time in which you experienced true Christian community. Has this been a regular, intermittent, or rare event in your life?

4. To whom are you currently accountable for progress in your spiritual life? How is that responsibility being divided amongst groups and individuals?

5. In what realm or relationship do you realize the need for greater community? What "chaos" are you resisting? What fears lie behind this?

Getting Started

On Your Own

Personal assessment in the area of accountability and guidance is notoriously unreliable. Most of us are skilled at self-deception. Invite another disciple to spend some time with you to examine your current relationships and commitments. Are you presently involved in a group that is challenging you sufficiently? To whom is the inner reality of your life with God regularly laid bare? Who has permission to help you hear God's voice for your life, and to speak to you about that frankly? Pray together and formulate any needed steps to deepen your experience of "Antioch."

As a Congregation

In baseball, three strikes and you're out. When it comes to starting a small group ministry in a church, three strikes and you're about average. What is your congregation's history of small group ministry? What have been the false starts and the greatest successes? Most importantly: In what ways would small, intentional gatherings of disciples be crucial to the fulfillment of your vision?

If small groups are not already a key component in your church, enter a season of study (at least six months) to discern God's leading in this area.

WHERE IS YOUR MACEDONIA?

On September 11, 2001, United Airlines Flight 93 crashed in western Pennsylvania, well short of the presumed target of its terrorist hijackers. After passengers learned through AirFone conversations that other jets had been used that morning as guided missiles, they began to formulate a plan. They knew the reality of their situation. Thirty-eight-year-old Tom Burnett, executive of a medical research company, called his wife and said, "All of us are going to die." Then Burnett said something else. Everyone on the plane was going to die, but "some of us are going to do something about it."

That's compelling theology. All of us are going to die. But before we die, what are we willing to do? What do we intend to do with the incredible gift of life that God has given to us?

The passengers on Flight 93 had just moments to answer that question. Most of us assume we have a lifetime. Maybe at the next important crossroads we will do the right thing. That's when we'll make the hard choice. But the longer we wait, the fewer opportunities remain before us. The chance to make a difference begins to slip right through our fingers.

"Come Over and Help Us"

Year after year the apostle Paul arrived at crossroads where the shape of his life and the direction of his ministry could have gone one way or the other. He stood at one such juncture in the seaport city of Troas. Paul had never been this far from home. As we learn from Acts 16:6–10, he had utilized his second missionary journey as an opportunity to revisit and encourage those who had come to know Christ on his first trip. Then he turned toward the west.

Apparently Paul planned to follow the Via Sebaste to Ephesus, Roman capital of the province of Asia. But he was "kept by the Holy Spirit from preaching the word" there. Paul and his companions veered to the north, toward the strategic Black Sea ports of Bithynia, "but the Spirit of Jesus would not allow them to." We do not know precisely how the Spirit directed Paul on these occasions. But he must have wondered where God was taking him. Before him lay the Aegean Sea and, beyond that, Greece and Rome.

One night in Troas, "Paul had a vision of a man of Macedonia standing and begging him, 'Come over to Macedonia and help us.' After Paul had seen the vision, we got ready at once to leave for Macedonia, concluding that God had called us to preach the gospel to them" (Acts 16:9,10). How exactly did Paul experience this vision? We do not know. Who was the mysterious man from Macedonia? Commentators have had a field day. It's hard to overlook the sudden change of pronoun in verse 10: "After Paul had seen the vision, we got ready at once..." For the first time, the author of the book of Acts is writing autobiographically. From this point on Luke is traveling with Paul & Company. Many have suggested that Luke himself was the man from Macedonia who pleaded with Paul in the vision to "come over and help us."

Regardless of the vision's identity, the significance of this moment cannot be overstated. When Paul sailed for Macedonia he was leaving familiar territory. He was changing forever the boundary of his comfort zone. In the *Expositor's Bible Commentary*, New Testament scholar Richard N. Longenecker writes, "Authentic turning points in history are few. But surely among them that of the Macedonian vision ranks high. Because of Paul's obedience at this point, the gospel went westward; and ultimately Europe and the Western world were evangelized. Christian response to the call of God is never a trivial thing. Indeed, as in this instance, great issues and untold blessings may depend on it" (Vol. 9, Zondervan, 1981, p. 458).

Being and Doing

None of us is going to get out of this world alive. We all are going to die. But some of us, by God's grace, can do something in the meantime. What are you willing to do?

Where is your Macedonia? What is the mission field that is just beyond your comfort zone? Where is the place that you suspect God wants you to go—farther than any place you have been before? Perhaps you've pictured yourself going there—if time, money, safety, and "common sense" weren't such issues. Until we trust that God is in this call, and step out in faith that he himself will meet us on the far shore, Macedonia will haunt us as long as we live.

The odds are strong that your Macedonia will not turn out to be an actual place. You won't have to pack a suitcase, get your shots, and travel halfway around the world. God is faithful to give us gifts and passions that we can apply to relationships and opportunities that are already at hand. It's also likely that your Macedonia will change from time to time. Most Christians experience God's call on their lives as a series of steps and transitions into a number of interrelated ministries. This is good news for those who have served as chaperones for the middle school overnight lock-in. God *will* extend a new call on your life…someday.

Furthermore, it's likely that the place where God wants you to serve is outside the walls of your church. God is certainly at work in and through the ministries of congregations. But a majority of us can expect to find our Macedonia beyond church walls—wherever kids, or teenagers, or neighbors, or whole people groups have a need that God has uniquely equipped us to meet.

Before we set sail in Macedonia's direction, however, we must know why we are taking this trip.

Many churches get stuck in the quicksand of the Frank Sinatra Syndrome—*do be do be do*. You know: You *do* something for God, while at the same time you aim to *be* something for God, and it doesn't matter which comes first. The Bible says, however, that there is an order. *Being* comes first. The only way I can do world-changing ministry is to know that *I am blessed* and chosen by God. I don't first *do* something to earn God's attention or affection. Doing always comes second. In other words, I am not traveling to Macedonia to "find myself," but to bless others in response to the blessing that I have received from God.

The Tools for the Task

In order to make a difference in Macedonia we will need special tools. God insists on giving them to us, for free.

When Paul addresses the subject of doing ministry in I Corinthians 12, he begins with two "being" statements. In verse 7 he writes, "Now to each one the manifestation of the Spirit is given for the common good." After itemizing some spiritual gifts, Paul then says in verse 11, "All these are the work of one and the same Spirit, and he gives them to each one, just as he determines."

These two statements have important similarities. Both tell us that spiritual gifts are the *Holy Spirit's* supernatural tools for doing ministry. Therefore we're not talking about genetic endowments or

acquired abilities or the results of fitness programs, personal train-
ers, or spiritual steroids.

Both of these verses also tell us who is on the receiving end
of spiritual gifts. "Each one" means every individual who has ever
enrolled as a disciple of Jesus. If you are a disciple, then you are
charged with helping make other disciples. And since that is the
essence of the Great Commission given to us by Jesus, you have
received a spiritual gift to help you help others.

Both verses also tell us *how* spiritual gifts arrive. They are given.
The Greek word for gift is *charis*, which is frequently translated
"grace." There's a short but important list in the Bible of things
that God insists on giving. They can never be earned and they can
never be deserved. In John 3:16 we read, "God loved the world so
much that he gave his only Son." Ephesians 1:7 declares, "In him
we have redemption through his blood, the forgiveness of our sins."
Ephesians 2:8, 9 says, "For it is by grace that you have been saved,
and not because of things you have done." I Corinthians 12 assures
us that spiritual gifts are exactly as advertised—they are *gifts* that
God gives to every one of his children.

To summarize, what do we know about the best things in life?
The best things in life are not things. The best things in life come
from God. And God insists on simply giving us these things as his
gifts. In his book, *Hustling God*, Craig Barnes says that grace is
like getting the job you've always wanted, receiving a 100 percent
clean bill of health on your physical, and then hearing your child
say, "Mommy, someone named Ed McMahon is standing at our front
door holding an envelope"—and all that happening on the same day.
"Every morning we wake up to a world we did not create to enjoy
a relationship with God we could not possibly earn" (Zondervan,
1999, p. 121).

Deep in our hearts, God has planted a hunger to reclaim that
world. God's world has been lacerated by sin. He has wired us in

such a way that we want to make a difference. We dream of being significant. Here's the hard question: Are we willing to accept from God the resources to accomplish this, when we know we don't deserve them?

We are very strange people. In one part of our heads we know that God can do anything. God can make the Crab Nebula, and God can fashion the intricate workings of a semipermeable cell membrane, and God can invent more than 600,000 species of beetles. But another part of us says, "It's all up to me. I have to do the hard work. God shouldn't have to *give* me something."

You Get to Carry the Ball

Nor do we find it easy to believe that God is willing to use us—*every one of us*— to build his kingdom. There has to be a catch.

On most top-drawer football teams only a few performers ever get to touch the ball. They are the so-called money players. Everybody else on the team accepts a supporting role. Realistically the money players are the only team members who are likely to score or radically affect the outcome of a game. Each year at the time of the Super Bowl, even after a week of saturation news coverage, most football fans can name only six or eight of the 100 or so players who have suited up for the game. Are you an offensive lineman? You'd better stop dreaming about getting a pregame interview with ESPN.

Whenever churches imitate this "star system" that is so typical of professional sports, we find ourselves in big trouble. We start to imagine that only a few people are spiritually capable of carrying the ball. We've identified our own money players. There's the preacher, of course. And the soprano soloist. Don't forget the missionary, or the major donor who becomes the go-to-guy when the money is tight. And don't overlook that one mom who is always willing to chaperone the middle school overnight lock-in. These are the people who do great things for God. The rest of us watch and pray. What we pray is that they all aren't transferred in the same month.

Is that picture found anywhere in the Bible? Of course not. What God's Word tells us is that every disciple is called to make a difference. If you are a lifelong learner of Jesus Christ, then you get the ball. In fact, you're called to score. The plain truth is that every follower of Jesus is expected to do great things for God—to radically affect the growth of God's kingdom through his or her presence and faithfulness.

That's the gist of what Paul says in I Corinthians 12:12: "The body is a unit, though it is made up of many parts; and though all its parts are many, they form one body." Paul summarizes in verse 27: "Now you are the body of Christ, and each one of you is a part of it."

Contemporary biologists have learned that it's a big deal even to be a very small part of a living body. Every cell in a living organism has exactly the same DNA—the unique genetic signature of that particular creature. If you're part of the Body of Christ, God has implanted discipleship DNA in your heart and your mind. Biologists know that they can take the DNA from any cell in a living thing, regardless of its function, and from it alone they can reproduce an entirely new, healthy organism. In the same way, if the mission statement of what Jesus is trying to accomplish is written on our hearts, God could theoretically work through any one of us as he worked through Paul—breaking ground on a whole new project of spiritual reclamation.

Pastors may be ministers with a capital *m*, but everyone who has made a commitment to Christ is at least a minister with a lower case *m*. As members of his Body, we all are charged with doing the work of Jesus—bringing, equipping, and sending out new disciples into this broken world. *All of us get to carry the ball.*

Your Gift Matters

There's a story about a woman who found herself in a precarious position. She locked her keys in her car in a threatening part of town, only a few minutes before a crucial appointment. She called the police, but the dispatcher said, "Ma'am, I'm sorry, but we can't send anyone your way for at least forty minutes." Quickly she prayed, "Lord, I believe you want me at that appointment. Please send me a good man to get me back into my car." At that very instant an intimidating-looking fellow in a motorcycle jacket walked around the corner. After sizing up the situation he said, "Lady, do you need some help?" Thirty seconds later her car door was open.

Immediately she offered a prayer of thanks: "Lord, thank you for sending me a good man!" When he heard that prayer the guy in the leather jacket looked sheepish. "Sorry to disappoint you, lady, but I'm not exactly a good man. In fact, right now I'm out on probation for grand theft auto." The woman reflected on that for a moment, and then offered a second prayer: "Thank you, Lord, for sending me a professional."

Unfortunately, this is the strategy of the ABC church. We're not sure if our rank-and-file members are "good enough" to do authentic ministry, but at least we've got some professionals. We take the mission of the church and hire it out to a handful of specialists who will perform it on our behalf.

Has God ever, in any generation, called or equipped one amazingly overextended person to take on 100 different ministry roles? Let's put it this way: Do you know what a rhetorical question is? History bears witness that God regularly calls 100 people to assume one role each. In *Doing Church as a Team*, Wayne Cordeiro points out that traditionally the pastor is expected to do the whole ministry of a particular church and to recruit God's people to help him or her. But the Bible clearly teaches that it's the other way around. All of God's people have been spiritually enlisted to do the work of ministry—and to get the pastor to help *them*! (Regal Books, 2000, p. 48).

Being disciples who make other disciples isn't the responsibility of a few individuals. That is the sacred call of every follower of Jesus. But what if we're convinced that our gifts and our roles are, for all intents and purposes, irrelevant, and are never going to make a lasting impact for the kingdom? Paul writes in verses 15 and 16: "If the foot should say, 'Because I am not a hand, I do not belong to the body,' it would not for that reason cease to be part of the body. And if the ear should say, 'Because I am not an eye, I do not belong to the body,' it would not for that reason cease to be part of the body."

The Right Place at the Right Time

God refuses to let us define ourselves by what we cannot do. Maybe within the last week you've said, "I don't have the performance gifts that other people have. I can't pray out loud, so don't ask me to do that. And I could never teach a Bible story to a child. I'm terrified of walking into a critical care situation and spending time with someone who's just gotten bad news. *I can't do anything.*"

Remember Paul's words: "Now to each one the manifestation of the Spirit is given for the common good." If you trust Christ, then the Holy Spirit has strategically given you at least one spiritual gift in an area where your church needs you to be carrying the ball right now.

How do we discover our personal spiritual gifts? Your process almost certainly will involve prayer, Bible study, and talking openly with those who know your heart well. An Antioch-like group would be ideal. You may choose to take a spiritual gift inventory. Pay attention to what activities prompt your deepest experiences of joy, and do some personal field-testing of a variety of ministry options.

115

What if a long period of time has gone by, and you still haven't identified your spiritual gift? Don't despair. We don't need to know at every moment exactly what God is accomplishing through us. All we need to do is keep trusting and obeying him. As long as we keep doing that, we'll end up in the right places at the right times.

Risking Our Gifts for God

When God places a Macedonia on our hearts—an arena of service beyond our current levels of comfort and experience—God is faithful to give us the supernatural tools that we will need. One further element is required. *We need to risk going forward.*

In the parable of the three servants in Matthew 25:14–30 Jesus informs us that the day will come when each of us will have a conversation with him about what we did with our lives—about what we did with the gifts, resources, and opportunities that we each received. We will talk with him about whether we chose to give or to take, to step out or to hold back, to risk or to hoard, to live as his servant or to masquerade as our own master. When we heard the call to sail to Macedonia did we linger on *terra firma* or did we choose to trim the sails? What we discover in the parable is that this next-world conversation has several possible outcomes, and that the only person who can speak for your future is *you*.

The details of the story are familiar. The first servant immediately goes to work investing and risking the five talents he has received. At his accountability interview he presents an additional five talents. He receives his reward in verse 21: "Well done, good and faithful servant. You have been faithful with a few things; I will put you in charge of many things."

An identical experience awaits the servant who multiplies the two talents that he is given. Notice that the master doesn't say, "So why didn't you come up with five talents?" God's rewards are based on the resources that he provides us, not on resources that we don't have. The master is primarily focused on the degree to which we are willing to step out, to trust him, and to take risks for the sake of advancing his interests.

That becomes clear when we arrive at verse 24, which is Jesus' conversation with the third servant. This cautious fellow says to the master, "I know that you are a hard man, harvesting where you have not sown and gathering where you have not scattered seed. So I was afraid and went out and hid your talent in the ground. See, here is what belongs to you." And it is evident at this moment that the third servant expects applause. He awaits his attaboy. His mission is accomplished: Despite everything that could possibly have gone wrong (buying Enron stock comes to mind) at least he didn't fail. He made sure of that.

The surprise of a lifetime comes next. "Why didn't you at least put my money on deposit with the bankers, so that when I returned I would have received it back with interest?" Why is the master so angry? Not because the servant was a management failure. In fact, failure would have been fine. Failure would have implied that some action had been taken. God is not disappointed when his servants fail; God is disappointed when his servants choose not to step out.

Henry Stanley is chiefly remembered as the American journalist who, in 1871, having walked into a jungle clearing in central Africa, spotted a single, pale-skinned man and said, "Dr. Livingstone, I presume?" In his own right, however, he was also a fearless explorer of uncharted territory in Africa. Until Stanley's extraordinary 1876 expedition it is assumed that no one—either inside or outside Africa—had ever been all the way down the treacherous Congo River, with its canyons, gorges, and cannibals. His trip took 999 days and was filled with unimaginable hardships.

One night the difficulties were so extreme that Stanley realized he had to make a choice—either to keep going forward into the unknown, or to head back toward security. That night he approached his friend and helper Frank Pocock. "Now Frank, my son, sit down. I am about to have a long and serious chat with you. Life and death—yours and mine—hang on the decision I make tonight." What did they do?

Pocock and Stanley decided to flip a coin—an Indian rupee. Heads they would go forward; tails they would go home. The coin came up tails. Disappointed, they flipped the coin again. Tails. "How about three out of five?" Once again it was tails. In fact the coin came up tails six times in a row. The two men decided to draw straws—long straw to go forward, short straw to go back. Every time they drew, however, they picked the short straw.

Stanley and Pocock finally realized that they had already made their decision. No matter what the coins or the straws "told them," in their hearts all they wanted to do was head down the Congo River into the Great Unknown. And so they did, making history in the process.

We don't have to flip coins or draw straws to know what is on the heart of Jesus. He has already told us. "Go into all the world and preach the good news to all creation" (Mk 16:15). Go where you have never gone before. Go to the Macedonia that God keeps laying on your heart.

In Jesus' story, the third servant plays it safe. He weighs all of his options and decides that stepping out, sharing what he has, sacrificially going to work on behalf of the master's interests, is too risky. It will cost too much. He even rationalizes that he has done the master a favor by not losing what he has been given. Ironically, in the end, what does it cost him not to go forward? It costs him everything. And what did he miss? He missed the chance to change the world. By saying yes to the call of God, disciples change the course of history all the time...and often don't even know it.

Are You Ready?

Twenty-seven years ago I met Ed Orme. We were both students at Purdue University, majoring in biology. Both of us grew up in Indianapolis and loved spelunking in southern Indiana caves. We lived in one of the most primitive dwelling places known to mankind—Purdue's Cary Quad—and seemed to be in a competition as to who could ride the junkiest bike on campus. We both loved the techno rock group Emerson, Lake & Palmer. It was cool listening together to ELP's song, "Are You Ready?" because it began, "Are you ready, Eddie, ready to rock and roll?"

Ed was fun. He was one of the most generous individuals I have ever known. He also could be crafty. One night, shortly after I announced my engagement to Mary Sue, Ed came to my dorm room on the pretext of getting some class notes. From the smile on his face I knew something was up. In fact he had led to my room a band of our common friends. Whenever I read the account of Judas leading the band of soldiers into the Garden of Gethsemane I can almost picture Ed's face. That evening I was tied up, blindfolded, covered with syrup and feathers, and left outdoors with a sign that simply read, "Engaged."

Most significantly, Ed and I both were young Christians. We both believed that we had been called by God. My call led me to establish a church a whole fifteen miles from the neighborhood where I grew up. Ed's call took him to the ends of the earth. Ed and his wife Sue became passionately committed to frontier missions—specifically to bringing the good news of Jesus Christ to Muslims, one of the most challenging gospel harvest fields in the world.

They trained for years to live in Pakistan, learning the native tongues, one of which was Urdu. Ed and I thought it was a riot that he had gone to Purdue and now spoke Urdu. He was brilliant at it. They moved to Karachi, raised four sons, and in the course of a decade and a half, through incredible patience, prayer, love, and deep trust in God, brought several households of Muslims to Christ. God was using Ed to make a difference in Pakistan.

The song said, "Are you ready, Eddie?" Ed was ready—ready to live and to die for the people of Pakistan, for the sake of Christ. And that is what he did, at age 46. Ed contracted a strain of malaria that took his life before he could get the medical help that might have saved him.

The memorial service was conducted in Indianapolis. An open microphone was provided so that people might stand and witness to the work of God in their lives through Ed Orme. The service lasted two-and-a-half hours. As I took my seat I looked to the right and noticed that I was just one chair away from a well known Christian speaker. The previous year I had worked and waited for eleven months to bring him on a visit to our church. This same man had now traveled all the way from his home in California just to take his turn at the mike and speak about Ed for five minutes.

Those of us at the service could feel that our old, comfortable understandings of the world were being deconstructed. We were being challenged. Our hearts for Christ and for his work were growing. It was all because Ed had faithfully answered God's call to serve.

We're all going to die. But some of us, by God's grace, are going to do something in the meantime. Are you ready? Will you risk what God has given to you for the sake of Macedonia?

Questions for Further Exploration

Personal, one-on-one, or small groups

1. If resources were unlimited, what would you most like to do for the sake of Jesus Christ?

2. In your view, is your ministry dream in question #1 really limited by resources? What is keeping you from going forward?

3. "You get to carry the ball." Has your church delivered this message to every member? What percent believe it? What percent are living it?

4. Is your Macedonia within the walls of your church, or outside? Do you expect this to change in the future?

5. When was a time that you knew that you obeyed the call of God? When was a time that you resisted?

Getting Started

On Your Own

Spiritual gift inventories have become a proven way to help discern a sense of God's calling to ministry. If you haven't taken such an inventory within the past two years, it is wise to do so again—even as an affirmation of what you are already doing. Many such tools are available. It is helpful to choose a different inventory from a Christian bookstore or one that might be available on-line.

As a Congregation

Gather a group of church leaders or members to pray and reflect on this question: *Whom, right now, can we picture calling to us, "Please come and help us"?* Try to discern what group, or neighborhood, or mission field, or cause is waiting for your church to come forward and enter a radical new expression of ministry.

What will you do with the responses that you receive?

PART II

THE SIX MARKS OF A DISCIPLE

Being disciples who make disciples is the need of this and every hour. What kinds of disciples do we have in mind? What should the typical, healthy follower of Jesus look like? What qualities and behaviors—regardless of background, context, generation, or geography—ought to characterize the life of one seeking to be entirely like the Son of God?

An acceptable profile would have to be *biblical* (that is, an accurate reflection of Jesus' own teaching); *simple* (understandable by adults and children alike); *teachable* (easy to grasp and a cinch to memorize); *practical* (useful for a disciple's self-evaluation); *balanced* (respectful of all of the historical schools of Christian thought and practice that have informed us of the richness of what it means to follow Jesus); and *visionary* (able to serve as the benchmark and the curriculum for everything a congregation might attempt to do and to be).

The profile that I have come to embrace is called the "Six Marks of a Disciple." It embodies the following characteristics of the man or the woman who is learning to live like Jesus:

A Heart for Christ Alone
A Mind Transformed by the Word
Arms of Love
Knees for Prayer
A Voice to Speak the Good News
A Spirit of Servanthood and Stewardship

Realistically we could propose twelve marks—or twenty-four or thirty-six. I believe these half-dozen, however, to be the least common denominators of Christian discipleship. On the one hand, all the other attributes of healthy spirituality can be contained within them; on the other hand, further reductions would do violence to the Gospel.

The six marks represent the essence and the *raison d'etre* for the six relationships we have already explored. To what end do we have a mentor, an apprentice, an accountability group, and a mission field? All are directed to the embodiment of these discipleship characteristics, to the glory of God. Therefore, the marks are never far from our minds whenever we consider the relationships, and we never cease thinking about the relationships as the primary means by which we grow into the reality of the marks.

As the following chapters explore each mark, there will be five arenas that are particularly deserving of our attention:

Vision. What exactly do we mean by this characteristic? We will consider Jesus' uncompromising teaching on this aspect of followership.

Crisis. How does the embodiment of this mark make us countercultural in the extreme? We will discuss the gigantic obstacles to living like Jesus in the twenty-first century.

Gaps. What paradigm shifts will have to happen in my life in order to move from seeker, to spiritual beginner, to intermediate, to mature disciple in this realm of becoming like Christ? You will see that each mark addresses an inner hunger, and calls us to embark on a unique journey.

Responsibility. What will my obedience mean to God, and what will my faithfulness in this area mean to fellow disciples? We will discover that each mark implies a double accountability.

Resources. What tools and tactics are available for individuals, small groups, and congregations to make progress? Here we will learn how the six primary relationships make all the difference.

8

A HEART FOR CHRIST ALONE

Jesus, as the one-and-only Son of God, becomes the
priority in all of life; we worship him with all our
heart, mind, soul and strength.

*"If anyone comes to me and does not hate his father
and mother, his wife and children, his brothers and
sisters—yes, even his own life—he cannot be my
disciple. And anyone who does not carry his cross
and follow me cannot be my disciple."*

(Luke 14:26–27)

The first mark of the authentic disciple is a heart for Christ alone. The other five marks may be encountered in almost any sequence, but the first mark simply has to be first. Its priority cannot be negotiated. The life that is lived well must be organized around a foundational certainty that Jesus alone is the Giver of Meaning to human existence.

No Rival Gods

Jesus consistently presented himself as the most crucial aspect of reality. "I am the bread of life" (Jn 6:35). "I am the resurrection and the life. He who believes in me will live, even though he dies" (Jn 11:25). "I and the Father are one" (Jn 10:30). It is consistent with historic Christian theology to declare that Jesus Christ is reality. If the greatest goal of life is to be in step with what is real, then our most strategic commitment would be to invest a lifetime in the growing and nurturing of a core commitment to the one who alone is reality in the flesh. To ignore this or to refuse this is to be out of step with reality. It is literally to be insane.

Of course modernity has its own take on what constitutes insanity. A heart for Christ alone will never make sense to the world. It can never be pursued in a "half-hearted" fashion. The first mark of the disciple, therefore, represents a full-blown departure from the voices, currents, and values of the society that surrounds us.

In our day to ask an aspiring disciple to grow a heart for Christ *alone* seems puzzling, unreasonable, and downright rude. Jesus himself never asked for anything less. "I am the way, the truth and the life; no one comes to the Father except through me" (Jn 14:6). In Luke 14:26–27 he made it abundantly clear that unless our fidelity to him is *prior and superior* to every other relationship or aspiration life has to offer, including the deepest levels of our own self-interest, we are disqualified from discipleship before we even begin.

Throughout Scripture God thunders that he will tolerate no rival deities, no alternative truth systems. "This is what the Lord says—Israel's King and Redeemer, the Lord Almighty: I am the first and I am the last; apart from me there is no God. Who then is like me? Let him proclaim it. Let him declare and lay out before me what has happened since I established my ancient people—and what is yet to come—yes, let him foretell what will come. Do not tremble, do not be afraid. Did I not proclaim this and foretell it long ago? You are my witnesses. Is there any God besides me? No, there is no other Rock. I know not one" (Is 44:6–8). Like a jealous lover God shatters the notion that a cafeteria-style approach to spiritual truth is somehow noble and enlightened.

Jesus says in John 15:5, "I am the vine, you are the branches. If a man remains in me and I in him, he will bear much fruit." If Jesus had stopped at the end of that sentence he would hardly raise an eyebrow in today's world. Jesus was claiming a special authority to nourish people spiritually. That makes him one of hundreds of claimants, including Mohammed, Krishna, Mary Baker Eddy, Buddha, Sun Myung Moon, David Koresh, and numerous others. In India alone there are as many as 300 million "local" deities.

With his next statement, however, Jesus draws a line in the sand: "Apart from me you can do nothing." Who does he think he is? Jesus isn't merely claiming a share of the world's spiritual power; he's announcing that spiritual power begins and ends with him alone. Just to make sure we understand this claim, he continues, "If anyone does not remain in me, he is like a branch that is thrown away and withers; such branches are picked up, thrown into the fire and burned." It's not just that choosing Jesus is a good thing— *not choosing Jesus* is a catastrophic thing.

We're not surprised when religious leaders say, "Follow me and I'll teach you how to find the truth." Jesus says, "I *am* the truth" (Jn 14:6). Other religious leaders say, "Join up with me and I'll help you become enlightened." Jesus says, "I *am* the light of the world" (Jn 8:12). Other leaders promise, "Follow me and I will show you the many doors to God." Jesus says, "I *am* the door" (Jn 10:7). According to Jesus, the meaning of life is cultivating a heart for him *alone*.

Practical Atheism

One of the most notable features of contemporary culture, however, is its embrace of an opposite point of view. "Modernity" champions the idea that the presence of God, even the existence of God, is essentially irrelevant. Society hums along as if the reality of God is unnecessary for us to get through the next twenty-four hours. We don't need God in order to do our banking, job-searching, love-making, shopping or politicking. Ignoring the claims of God's Son has become no big deal. Tens of thousands of small details make up our lives—and if we happen to address them without a single reference to Jesus of Nazareth, *there is no reason to believe that we are somehow less than whole.*

One of the subtle temptations in America today is to live, for all intents and purposes, as an atheist. Even in our churches God seems "weightless." There is a spirit of familiarity with God in our worship services, but little sense of trembling and awe. The Creator is seldom pictured as "high and lifted up," searingly holy, or surrounded by "glory" (a translation of the Hebrew word *kaboth*, which in part means "weight"). God and God's Son are rarely honored as the weightiest realities in our hearts.

Therefore few challenges are tougher for would-be disciples in the twenty-first century than affirming the "onlyness" of Jesus. Even to *ask* for such a commitment is to risk serious misunderstanding. Why are we so out of touch with the spirit of our times? How can we dare preach that loyalty to Christ should exclude other perspectives and opinions about spiritual reality?

In the fall of 2003 the Canadian Parliament received Bill C-250. If passed, the Bible would be classified as hate literature, owing to the fact that certain biblical passages appear to speak against protected classes in the "hate propaganda" section of the country's criminal code (Alice Martin & Jenni Parker, *Crosswalk.com*, October 2003).

When its spiritual sourcebook is decried as inherently hateful, the Church is facing a cultural crisis indeed.

The story is told about a certain man who, on his way to work every morning, walked past a clockmaker's store. It was part of his daily ritual to pause long enough to gaze at the big grandfather clock standing in the shop window. One day the clockmaker, who had noticed this behavior, stepped outside and struck up a conversation. "This one's a real beauty, isn't she?" he said, pointing to the clock in the window.

"I'll say," said the man on the street. "To tell you the truth, I actually have another motive for stopping here every day. I'm the timekeeper at the local factory. It's my job to blow the whistle at precisely four o'clock. This wristwatch of mine is notoriously unreliable, so every day I stop and recalibrate it with this magnificent timepiece of yours."

"Is that so?" said the clockmaker, who was beginning to feel a bit uneasy. "I hate to tell you this, but the reason this grandfather clock doesn't sell is that I've never been able to make it work precisely right. In fact I readjust it every single day—right at four o'clock, when I hear the whistle go off at your factory!"

Life's most important questions are pretty simple: What time is it right now, and who has the authority to say so? Our culture has answered resoundingly: *There is no Greenwich mean time when it comes to the meaning of life.* There is no final authority. Everyone winds his own watch and marches to his own schedule.

A couple of years ago I came up behind a car driven by a teen-aged girl. I noticed its bumper sticker: *Galileo was wrong; the world revolves around ME.* In today's world that makes laughably perfect sense. If there is nothing outside myself that is eternally valid or true, then the question of where I will get my rules for living is a no-brainer. The world revolves around *me.* "Truth" is what turns out to be true for me. My feelings, my perspectives, and my take on reality become reality itself.

In today's world the cereal aisle in the grocery store, fully stocked with an array of colorful options both old and new, is the metaphor for spiritual decision-making. Individuals demand the right to make choices. As Mike Starkey writes in his book *God, Sex, and the Search for Lost Wonder*, "If theology is the study of God (from the Greek word *theos*), then most contemporary spirituality is 'me-ology,' the art of taking my own tastes, preferences and moods and creating a customized religion just for me" (InterVarsity Press, 1998, p. 115).

Jesus invites us down a different path. "Come and follow me," he says. To do so is to begin a journey of surrender.

Closing the Gaps

One of the tasks of spiritual discernment is to identify the goal that Christ has set for us, to plant a flag where we are currently standing, and then to plot a course that will erase the distance between those two points. Closing the gaps in our experience and expression of the six marks takes a lifetime. Our imitation of Jesus won't be complete until our Lord himself finishes the process. "We know that when he appears, we shall be like him, for we shall see him as he is" (I Jn 3:2). Conceding the fact that we will never know the fullness of Christlikeness in this world, we are still called to move forward in partnership with the Holy Spirit with all of our energy.

A "gap analysis" of the first mark has to take into account the fact that success looks different at different levels of spiritual maturity. We have found it helpful to spotlight four stages on the path. The first is that of the seeker, the person who has not yet made a commitment to Christ. How ought we define growth in the first mark for someone who is seeking spiritual truth?

From: I am the leader of my own life.

To: I realize that I must let Jesus be the leader of my life.

According to the Bible, this is the decisive transaction of salvation. A seeker must believe the claims that Jesus made about himself

132

and then receive the gift of life that Jesus uniquely offers (Jn 1:12). In the process there is a change in leadership. As the old boss of my own life, I have to step aside. A new boss has access to the CEO's chair.

The Bible is patently clear about who does the work to bring this about. Every human being needs to be spiritually rescued, and no one is equipped to do the job for himself. Our relationship with God isn't just a little misaligned. Trying harder to please God is futile. What then about the popular option of trying much, much harder? Futile again. Every non-Christian religious option on the planet boils down to a do-it-yourself proposition. One way or another, we are summoned to deliver ourselves from trouble. Only Christianity proposes that help has to come from beyond ourselves.

The Hero from Out of Town

Dr. Dale Bruner is an exceptional Bible teacher. I once heard him make this point in a seminar, which I admit had never occurred to me: *In westerns, the hero always comes from out of town.* Common, hard-working people have made a mess of things, bad *hombres* have seized power, and now a stranger has to arrive on the scene to set things right.

I decided to do what Dr. Bruner had done, which is to see for myself if this is really true. I went to the video store and rented *Shane*, a classic western from the 1950s. The movie opens with a small, homesteading family set against a magnificent Rocky Mountain backdrop. The little boy in the family looks up and sees a lone rider approaching the homestead. He speaks the opening words of the movie: "Someone's comin', Pa."

Alan Ladd, in the role of Shane, moseys up and says, "Hope you don't mind my cutting through your place." Before ten minutes go by the bad guys—the Ryker gang—have appeared on the scene. They look suspiciously at Alan Ladd and snarl, "Who are you, stranger?"

That's it. The entire plot of the movie has been laid out in less than ten minutes. We have disputed property, bad guys with guns, and a stranger who will ultimately save the day.

Does this formula work for cartoon westerns? Check out *Feivel Goes West*, where an ethnic mouse from lower New York City heads west to clean up a town run by very bad cats. How about comedic westerns? In *Shanghai Noon* Jackie Chan, the master of martial arts, comes all the way from China to beat up a few people in Carson City, Nevada, because they don't know how to solve their own problems.

Dr. Bruner pointed out that Americans don't seem to notice it, but every western tells the story of the Gospel. People on earth have problems. We've made a mess of things. We've surrendered our freedom to destructive powers. The solution has to come from somewhere else, from beyond ourselves. We need a hero from out of town.

That's what John says at the beginning of the book that bears his name. It is the account of how Jesus arrived in our world as a heroic stranger: "In the beginning was the Word, and the Word was with God, and the Word was God" (Jn 1:1). In John 1:10 we read, "He was in the world, and though the world was made through him, the world did not recognize him." Here is the affirmation that the Son of God came to earth as a stranger.

John continues, "He came to that which was his own, but his own did not receive him. Yet to all who received him, to those who believed in his name, he gave the right to become children of God—children born not of natural descent, nor of human decision or a husband's will, but born of God" (Jn 1:11–13).

The climax takes place in John 1:14: "The Word became flesh and made his dwelling among us." [Or *moved into the neighborhood*, as Eugene Peterson colorfully renders it in *The Message*, John 1:14.] "We have seen his glory, the glory of the One and Only, who came from the Father, full of grace and truth." Jesus came from out

134

of town—*way* out of town—in order to rescue an entire world of hurting people.

Loved by the "Losers"

In the Gospels we see that those who were most aware of their own need for rescue were the most welcoming of Jesus. They were drawn to him like filings to a magnet. People who saw themselves as spiritually "together," however, felt deeply threatened by Jesus. It goes against the flow. You'd think that if the holiest man on earth came to town, the ministers' association would throw him a catered dinner at the nicest country club, while all of society's rejects would keep a low profile. But that's not what happened. Jesus hung out with prostitutes, lepers, pagan soldiers, and a mixed-race woman who was five times divorced. They couldn't say enough nice things about him. The religious establishment held meetings to figure out how to liquidate him.

The truth is, we can't be healed until we admit ourselves to the ER. We have to join the group of spiritual "rejects" who say, "I have a problem that's way beyond band-aids." That places us exactly where God wants us, for what we learn in Scripture is that Jesus has already performed the radical procedure we most need by his death on the cross.

What are seekers asked to do? They are called to be "actively passive" in receiving the salvation that Jesus has accomplished—to surrender their own scepter so that the true King might begin a new reign. We are rescued not because we are clever or deserving or sacrificially industrious, but because God is gracious. If a misstep is made at this crucial juncture—if there is a fundamental misunderstanding in our minds as to why we are so privileged to have a relationship with Christ—then every other step on the journey will take us in the wrong direction.

A Journey of Surrender

A beginner in discipleship is someone who has received Jesus as both leader and forgiver, and recognizes that all this has happened because of grace. When it comes to embodying a heart for Christ alone, what is the gap that stretches out before a beginner?

From: Jesus is the leader of some aspects of my life.

To: Jesus is the leader of all aspects of my life.

If truth be told, most American churchgoers are beginners in the first mark of a disciple. That's because the Church at large has failed to demonstrate Christ's claim to lordship over everything— *and then to demand it as an absolute for the normal Christian life*.

A relationship with the Son of God has chiefly been portrayed as a journey of intellectual surrender. We are presented with a set of spiritual truth claims. We investigate their validity, become convinced of their veracity, and prayerfully acclaim Jesus as the rightful Lord of the universe. If a religious census were taken, we could now check the box that says "Christian." This is only the barest beginning, however, of what it means to have a heart for Christ alone.

Surrender must include every part of what it means to be human. The Christian subculture of America is increasingly blind to a creeping Gnosticism in both theology and practice. The earliest Christian heresies were Gnostic in flavor—that is, the mind was excessively valued above the body. Physicality was assumed to be a secondary arena for God's work, if indeed God cared at all for "that awful thing," my body. The Church's first theological giants joined to state the case that embodiment is the gift of God, who created the earth and our own bodies and pronounced them "good."

The spirit of our times, often associated with New Age philosophizing, is alive with Gnostic sensibilities. "True spirituality" concerns my inner life, not how I do the laundry. Progress in my life with God is attitudinal, emotional, ecstatic, or cerebral—not whether

I happen to help my neighbor clean out his garage. Contemporary spirituality, in other words, is assumed to be an invisible, personal, and internal experience. A number of Christians have falsely concluded that, if we give our intellectual assent to Jesus then what we do "on our own time"—commercially, physically, socially—is entirely up to us.

Paul, writing to an audience that had come under the influence of proto-Gnostic teaching, said, "And whatever you do, whether in word or deed, do it all in the name of the Lord Jesus, giving thanks to God the Father through him" (Col 3:17). The whole person belongs to God. All of life's details are to be brought under the Lordship of Jesus. How might this happen?

We can invite Jesus to take a walk with us, asking him to come alongside us during our routine visits to all our routine places. Ask Jesus to sit with you in the family room while you watch TV. Is the video that you have rented consistent with the life to which he has called you? Invite Jesus to look through your stock portfolio. Are your investments consistent with a kingdom perspective? Flip through the ledger of your checkbook and ask what he thinks about your purchases over the past thirty days. Ride with Jesus to your office. What does he think about your strategies to pull ahead of business competitors? Walk with him through your neighborhood, asking Jesus to let you see the people on your street through his eyes. What relationships need to be repaired? What acts of kindness have been deferred? Do my closets full of stuff, my calendar, my refrigerator, my reading list, and my recreation reflect a heart for the Son of God?

Surrendering leadership in every area of life is not a "been there, done that" experience. It is a process that never ends. Vigilance and intention can never be set aside. For instance, early in my walk with Christ I found it liberating and refreshingly easy to surrender my penchant for cursing. I have never been seriously tempted to take that ground back for myself. Another whole realm of speech, however, has defied all of my attempts at transformation. I enjoy delivering verbal zingers. Sometimes they are playful and welcome. Other times I hurdle across the boundary line of good judgment as if it's not even there. On those occasions my words can be cynical and wounding. Cultivating a heart for Christ alone in the way that I speak is to date a 30-year project. By God's grace I will be farther down the road thirty years from now.

Confronting Idolatry

Beyond the beginning stage of surrendering our lives to Christ's leadership we confront an intermediate gap. It looks like this:

From: Jesus may lead all of my life in accordance with my guidelines.

To: Jesus may lead all of my life in any manner he desires.

This distinction is subtle but telling. We cannot declare, "Lord, you are in charge of my love life," and then stipulate, "But remember, I *do want* a love life. Aloneness at this time…you know I can't handle that." God knows infinitely more than we can fathom. The journey of surrender at this point is not whether God is *there*. Nor is the primary issue whether God will be faithful. Our wrestling comes down to whether God's choices are *acceptable*. God will come through. But will we like what he delivers?

Apart from the doctrine of God the most frequently cited subject in the Bible is idolatry (by definition, whatever we might worship in lieu of God). Hideous idols of stone and precious metals are consistently easy to identify. The false God of my VISA card, however, has a pleasant and unassuming appearance. The idols of my most ancient dreams and prejudices are for all intents and purposes invisible to me—yet these are the malignant deities to which I bow most vigorously.

At this point I am almost powerless to self-diagnose my condition. Who can discern that vein of carefully concealed pride that makes me sigh, "This organization is lucky to have someone like me"? Who can call out the envy that I feel about the success of the guy down the street—and the insidious way that I attribute it to corner-cutting or superficiality instead of the blessing of God? Who can spot the poisoning effects of the hatred that still lurks in my spirit toward a family member who hurt me when I was a child?

Only a Barnabas-like mentor or a counselor who has permission to look into my life, or a group of trusted friends—presumably those who function as my Antioch—are strategically positioned to tell me the truth. *It is their call from God to tell me the truth.* I am capable of spiritual self-deception for the entirety of my days. Apart from sustaining redemptive relationships that include a primary element of accountability, "a heart for Christ alone" will never be anything more than a mantra. Christ's dominion over the core of my existence will never become a gift to share with the world.

We do of course share with the world whatever is in our hearts. Our Timothy will consciously or unconsciously imitate the degree to which we have surrendered control to Jesus. What we model screams louder than what we say. The watching world will study our responses and either see evidence that discipleship transforms a human life, or further confirmation that the church is a bastion of false advertising. We cannot fake what is at the center. "A good tree cannot bear bad fruit, and a bad tree cannot bear good fruit" (Mt 7:18).

Naming our false gods is where we begin. By the authority of the Word we must reveal the lies on which these idols are mounted, and then topple their authority by discovering, claiming, and living out the truth. Greed, for example, writes checks for security and significance that it cannot cash. Only God can keep the promises that money makes, and Jesus alone is worthy of our deepest trust. How might individuals and congregations confront this false god?

Affirming the truth is the first step. "You cannot serve God and Money" (Mt 6:24). An individual might choose to memorize this verse and to ponder its immediate ramifications. A church board might deploy one or two of its members to serve as "champions" of this concept, keeping it at the forefront of its meetings for at least one year. The second step is making a decisive break with the false god. Individuals might enter a stewardship training experience such as Crown Ministries, which has built-in applications at every step. A church board may need to rewrite its own by-laws and budgeting procedures to ensure that Jesus' perspective on finances is publicly honored. Finally, sustaining the Lordship of Christ requires ongoing accountability. An individual might find a few spiritual confidants who offer the gift of friendship and oversight. A board will need to schedule opportunities to literally stop and ask, "Are we doing what we set out to do? Is Christ being honored by our fiscal choices?" Confronting idols—reversing long-term patterns of believing spiritual lies—is not easy. But it is a work in which we can expect the most enthusiastic partnership of the Holy Spirit.

The Legacy of a Surrendered Life

And what of the person that we might describe as a mature disciple? There is still a gap to be closed:

From: I give my all to Jesus for my fulfillment.

To: I give my all to Jesus for his glory.

From beginning to end true spirituality is not about me. It is about the one who is Lord of everything. Here is the great irony: In allowing Christ to take his rightful spot at the core of my existence, I am enriched as never before. The greatest blessing comes not from seeking the blessing itself, but by nurturing an exclusive lifelong passion for the one who blesses. The legacy of such surrender is increased confidence in Christ—in life and in death.

Lyman Coleman, founder of the Serendipity small group resources that have blessed so many Christians over the past forty years, lost his wife Margaret in the fall of 2000. Months later Lyman sent out a letter in which he tried to put into words what he experienced over the ensuing winter:

> *I don't think the pain of losing Margaret hit me until I was driving back to Denver over New Year's weekend. This would have been three days of communion with my beloved. I found myself going into the little "watering holes" where we stopped along the way, and walking out without eating. In the next few weeks, I lost twenty-five pounds. I was afraid to go out. Read the mail. Answer the phone. Do anything. Fortunately, I live in a co-housing community where people notice if you are not there. Neighbors got on my case. One said, "You're going to make a choice in six months to live or die."*

As the letter continues Lyman describes the agonizing process of moving forward, of deciding whether or not his life was still worth living. He concludes:

> *With the money that people sent for a memorial, I bought hundreds of daffodil bulbs and gave them to the neighbors to plant. It has been a cold winter and the daffodils are still underground, but in a little while they will bloom in all of their glory. It has been a long winter for me, too. I feel like I don't belong anywhere. To anyone. I am lonely. Lost. But Easter is coming. We will be together again. Jesus promised it. I believe it. The daffodils will bloom again.*

Lyman Coleman chose to live. On what basis? That Jesus is not only alive, but is Lord of the universe. Therefore Margaret Coleman, follower of Jesus, is also still alive. Lyman has staked his life on that.

Will we stake our lives on Jesus' claim that he is the master of this world and the next? If so, there is no grander mission this day than to further deepen our heart for Christ alone.

Questions for Further Exploration

Personal, one-on-one, or small groups

1. Where would you place yourself in the "gaps" on this mark—as a seeker, a beginner, an intermediate, or a mature disciple?

2. Do you agree that the "onlyness" of Jesus as the way to know God feels like a scandal to contemporary people? What examples can you think of from your own experience?

3. Polls show that about 94 percent of Americans believe in God. Do you agree, nevertheless, that "practical atheism" rules the day—that most people are living as if there is no God?

4. What is your own experience of meeting Jesus? Was it a long-term process or a sudden development?

5. What is one area where you have substantially surrendered yourself to the leadership of Christ? What is one area where you continue to struggle?

Getting Started

On Your Own

A million dollars is on the line. Actually, let's raise the stakes. Eternity is on the line. The game show host leans toward you and says, "We need your final answer. Who exactly is Jesus Christ, and have you chosen to become his disciple for the rest of your life?" Write out your personal "final answer" to that two-part question.

What, if anything, is keeping your answer from being a final one? What questions or concerns need to be addressed? What do you plan to do about it?

As a Congregation

An idol is anything that receives the attention or honor that is due to Christ alone. At a gathering of church leaders or members, wrestle openly with this question: To what is our church bowing that is less than God? How did we get into this predicament? Are we willing to name the idol out loud, to deliberately turn away, and to give our full attention to the Lord?

What is our next step—and how should we go forward assuming that not everyone will identify the same idol?

9

A MIND TRANSFORMED BY THE WORD

We progressively come to view the world as God
views it, setting aside the world's values as our
minds are continually renewed by God's Word.

*"If you hold to my teaching, you are really my
disciples. Then you will know the truth,
and the truth will set you free."*

(John 8:31–32)

O
ne of the Christian leaders who emerged in Eastern Europe following the late-twentieth century collapse of communism has reflected, "For many years I knew what it meant to be ready to die for Jesus. Now I know what it means to have to live for Jesus. I can assure you: It is much harder to live for Jesus than to die for him."

It is hard to live for Jesus.

One reason is that our minds, shaped as they are by a culture that denies our need for active dependence on God, are not equal to the task. They are insufficiently steeped in the truth of God's Word.

We cannot "speak the truth in love" unless we know the truth. "The truth will set you free" will remain a tantalizing slogan unless we develop habits that help us both learn and act upon the commands of God. That finely crafted 23-minute Sunday sermon stands little chance against the tidal wave of a full week of advertising, sitcoms, HBO, billboards, teen magazines, the Internet, paperback novels, infomercials, and talk radio promulgating a message that is frequently antithetical to our own.

Consider our culture's obsessional dependence on screens for information, amusement, and guidance. In his book *All God's Children and Blue Suede Shoes* cultural critic Ken Myers writes, "Television is thus not simply the dominant medium of popular culture, it is the single most significant shared reality in our entire society. Christendom was defined as a region dominated by Christianity. Not all citizens of Christendom were Christians, but all understood it, all were influenced by its teaching, all institutions had to contend with it. Christianity was the one great assumption of Christendom. I can think of no entity today capable of such a culturally unifying role except television. In television, we live and move and have our being" (Crossways Books, 1989, p. 160).

Television has helped foster a sense of disconnectedness. We quickly move from one stimulating experience to the next. News broadcasts frequently rely on three words to link stories. The anchor says, "And now this." We've been talking about one thing. Now we're talking about the next thing. What we heard before has already become old news. *And now this:* Here's the new news. In a world that denies the existence of a final standard of truth, or even an interpretive grid that will help us to differentiate important facts from less important facts, who's to say which news items actually matter?

Lost in a Forest of Data

A friend of mine in northern Indiana took a walk in the woods not far from his home. It wasn't long before he realized that he had no idea where he was, nor even what direction he was walking. What came to mind were the wise words of his father, spoken years earlier: "When lost in the woods, son, you can always find north by looking at a tree. The moss always grows on the north side." Obediently he approached a large tree. To his dismay he discovered that there was moss growing all the way around. "Oh, my gosh," he cried, "I'm at the South Pole!"

In today's world the old markers are failing us. People are lost in an endless forest of data. Everything seems confusing. Which way do we go? Is one direction better than another? In the Information Age, there are too many variables to assess and too many things to know. We suspect that only a few things are worth knowing. But which things? This year at least 130,000 new books will be published. How many of those books will be "essential reading"? Whom should we trust to wade though the oceans of information so that we might discover what we truly need to know?

The Christian response to this quandary is the cultivation of a mind transformed by the Word. The Bible does not itemize the specific information required to accomplish every task in the modern world. But it does supply everything needed for any generation to live the "good life" according to the good God who has given us life as a gift.

Not Mastery, but Transformation

The Bible is the world's most amazing book. If 100,000 people buy copies of a new novel or the latest diet plan, those publications automatically attain the status of "bestsellers." The Bible, by comparison, has been the world's best-selling book every year since the invention of the printing press. More than one billion copies have been placed in circulation. This is a book like no other. This is a book we *ought* to know, inside and out.

But let's be honest. Even though there are an average of six Bibles per household in the United States, our collective ignorance of what is on its pages is astonishing. In the era of *People* magazine and multifaceted interactive Websites, this book, with its 2000 pages about archaic people groups (most of which no longer exist) and with no pictures, bar graphs, or factoids to help us along the way, seems too obscure and intimidating to be grasped.

Our aim, however, is not complete mastery. Few people in history have mastered the Bible's contents. The issue isn't knowledge as much as transformation—the recasting of our minds according to a perspective that is consistent with the mind of God. The process by which this takes place may be described as a journey of renewal.

Paul challenges his readers in Romans 12:2: "Do not conform any longer to the pattern of this world, but be transformed by the renewing of your mind." The English words "conform" and "transform" translate verbs from decidedly different Greek roots. "Conform" is derived from the noun *schema*, which to the Greeks referred to one's external, ever-changing appearance. Our *schema* is changed by something as simple as a new hairstyle. "Transform," on the other hand, derives from the Greek word *morphe*, which speaks of a person's or an object's unchanging true identity. According to this verse, authentic spiritual change is not a matter of adopting new habits or cosmetic alterations; we are called to be transformed ("metamorphosed") at the very core our being. The doorway to such change is the renewal, or making-new, of the mind.

"I Believe…"

How do we get started? We begin by noting that the typical spiritual seeker, in order to enter the Christian experience, has to close a serious information gap:

From: My understanding of the Jesus of the Bible is insufficient to make me want to give my life to him.

To: I know enough of the Jesus of the Bible to ask him to be the leader and forgiver of my life.

To the Jews who had believed him, Jesus said, "If you hold to my teaching, you are really my disciples. Then you will know the truth, and the truth will set you free" (Jn 8:31–32).

How do we come to have the spiritual freedom that Jesus promises? Let's work our way backward through those two verses. Freedom comes by knowing the truth. How do we know the truth? By discovering and "holding" to what Jesus taught. And where do we find what Jesus taught? There's only one source in the world that credibly claims to present the full message of Jesus: the Bible. There is a widely felt need for easier access to this book. "When's the movie version going to come out?" is the operative question of our time.

A few years back we presented a weeknight mini-course called The Bible for Dummies. What kind of people would be vulnerable or desperate enough to show up for a class with such a title? *All kinds* of people showed up—charter church members, brand new Christians, introverts, extroverts, skeptics, and veteran Bible students. Our experience is that there is an almost universal hunger for a better handle on the Word. Church leaders can no longer assume that when they say, "Please turn to the book of Ephesians," a majority of listeners even know where to start looking.

Spiritual seekers have a specific question: "If I make a commitment to Christ, what content is supposed to follow the two words *I believe?*" What is an appropriate summary of the vastness of Scrip-

149

ture? A statement of sufficient brevity and precision is called a creed, a term derived from the Latin word *credo*, which itself means, "I believe."

In his book *Speaking As One* Scott Hoezee points out that creeds aren't the private property of religious groups. Dr. Timothy Leary, the 1960s countercultural guru who advocated personal drug use, summarized his beliefs in three short phrases: *Tune In, Turn On, Drop Out*. The creed of the famous atheist Robert Ingersoll could be expressed in four sentences:

Happiness is the only good.
The place to be happy is here.
The time to be happy is now.
The way to be happy is to make others so.

(Eerdmans, 1997, p. 7-8)

Even "unbelievers" have something they believe in. Everyone must ask, "What is worth my ultimate loyalty? What creed is worth living for and what beliefs are worth dying for?" Lifelong learners of Jesus Christ are convinced that a mind continually exposed to the narrative, poetry, and proclamation of the Old and New Testaments will increasingly be able to distinguish what is eternally important from what is trivial.

Our dilemma, of course, is that the Bible is an enormous book. Those exploring the claims of Christianity need a "short version" they can wrap their minds around. Here we don't have to reinvent the wheel, since the Church has been working on this project for two millennia. I belong to a Christian tradition that recognizes and celebrates eleven historic statements of faith. Some are ancient and concise (*The Apostles' Creed* and *Nicene Creed*); some speak to most of the major facets of Christian thinking and living (*The Westminster Confession*); others have been written within our lifetimes.

In recent years Americans have been less excited about creeds than locating "the Bible's top ten verses" or presenting "The Roman Road to Salvation"—a handful of statements culled from Paul's letter to the church at Rome. The ultimate short version of the Bible is that hand-painted sign being waved in the stands during the nationally televised football game: *John 3:16*. What exactly do seekers need to know? They need to understand how and why Jesus claimed to be the eternally right answer to the question, *Who is Your Lord?* What that entails will vary from person to person. This we can say for sure: Knowing a few verses and reciting a few doctrines is not what Paul meant by renewal of the mind. That will require a much more comprehensive encounter with the Word.

Hitting the Highlights

Peter, writing to a group of beginners on the discipleship path, offered this counsel: "Like newborn babies, crave spiritual milk, so that by it you may grow up in your salvation" (I Pt 2:11). Here is the gap to be bridged:

From: The Bible is overwhelming.

To: I understand the Bible's basic story and teachings.

Getting to know the Bible is like becoming acquainted with a large, vibrant city. Let's consider Chicago, the third largest metro area in the United States. If we were complete strangers to Chicago, how might we go about the task of encountering the city?

We might start with a flyover. If you've been in a jet 35,000 feet above the Windy City, you have a preliminary understanding of the sheer size and complexity of the real estate. But looking out an airplane window could never be mistaken for "knowing" the city. To understand the look and the feel and the values of Chicago firsthand, we would have to drive down its streets and rub shoulders with its residents. That's the task of Bible study. A bird's-eye view isn't enough. Our call is to experience these pages ourselves.

How do we begin? Do we start with the first verse of Genesis and read straight through? Frankly, that would be like starting on the south side of Chicago and zigzagging up every single street and alley until we reach Evanston, Illinois, on its northern border. Could we possibly remember how to tell those streets apart, and discern which ones were most important, by the time we reached the end of our journey?

Perhaps this is the year that you determined that you would do it. Starting on January 1 you would read the Bible straight through and enjoy the last few paragraphs of the book of Revelation with Dick Clark on New Year's Eve. Most earnest Bible readers, however, "hit the wall" in the month of February about the time they encounter the Holiness Code of the book of Leviticus—also known as the Head Scratchers Department: "Don't boil a goat in its mother's milk," "Don't plant your field with two kinds of seed," and so forth.

Don't be discouraged if you have attempted the Great Bible Reading Expedition and failed. The Bible is a history book—it's a real story rooted in space and time that concerns real people—but it doesn't have be read sequentially in order to be understood. If you were visiting Chicago for the first time, the best advice would be to experience some of the highlights. Go to the Shedd Aquarium. Ride the elevator to the top of the Sears Tower. Wander around the Museum of Science and Industry. Get a cheeseburger and a shake at Ed Debevic's 1950s-style restaurant.

That's a workable plan for making your first visit to the Bible, too. Some chapters and stories are much more important and accessible than others. Go there first. At the end of this chapter is a list of the Bible's top forty "addresses" of well known and oft-cited texts. In your quest to get acquainted with Scripture, start by visiting the highlights.

Getting Behind the Scenes

Chicagoans don't hesitate to admit that one part of their city is the most strategic. It's the business district called The Loop. Christians identify a kind of spiritual "business district" in the Bible. It's the

New Testament—particularly the four biographies of Jesus that are known as the Gospels: Matthew, Mark, Luke and John. We cut our teeth in Bible study on those four books because they are the key to everything else. They alone inform us about Jesus, the Messiah foretold in the Old Testament. And they provide the context we need to understand the rest of the New Testament.

In his book *Hearing God* Dallas Willard writes to the person who adopts a Type A approach to getting through the whole Bible in one year: "You may enjoy the reputation...and you may congratulate yourself on it. But will you become more like Christ and more filled with the life of God? It is a proven fact that many who read the Bible in this way, as if they were taking medicine or exercising on a schedule, do not advance spiritually. It is better in one year to have ten good verses transferred *into the substance of our lives* than to have every word of the Bible flash before our eyes" (InterVarsity Press, 1999, p. 163).

With time we'll feel drawn to move away from the familiar texts to experience what is behind the scenes. If we really want to know Chicago, after all, we can't spend all our time in the lobby of the Adler Planetarium. We have to visit the historic districts of the city and experience the older neighborhoods where it's not unusual to step into an entirely different world just by crossing to the other side of a single street.

In the same way, Bible students make it their aim to learn about the "historic districts" of God's Word. That's why we'll want to read the prophets—to find out why Ezekiel lay on his left side for months on end just to make a memorable point. We'll want to travel with Paul and Timothy on their preaching missions and hear why envious politicians said, "These men are turning the world upside down!" We'll want to meet Samson, the guy with the six-pack abs but nothing upstairs. And ultimately we'll want to read for ourselves those amazingly specific regulations that God gave to Israel, which were really his way of saying, "If you want to get close to a holy God, here's how you have to live."

We don't have to undertake this quest by ourselves. In recent years the number of Bible study tools and opportunities has simply exploded. Centuries of Christian reflection are now only four clicks away on our computers. Our greatest asset, however, is the privilege of studying Scripture in community. Within our "Antiochs" we can join a cadre of fellow learners—either a small group that is working its way through a specific part of the Bible, or a larger presentation format that allows us to experience the fruits of someone else's study. A combination of those two strategies is particularly effective.

Longing for God's Commands

The journey of renewal calls for an ever-increasing personal engagement with God's revelation:

From: I often let the Bible inform my understanding and choices.

To: I passionately study the Bible, allowing it to shape the entirety of my understanding and choices.

According to the paradigm of Christianity, the quality of our spiritual life hinges on the way we answer the first two relationship questions: Who is my Lord? Who am I? Apart from a tenacious commitment to studying and obeying Scripture, our answers will be guesses at best—and self-serving daydreams at worst.

Numerous texts tell us that the Bible must be tenaciously consumed in order to shape our inner worlds. God told Joshua, "Do not let this Book of the Law depart from your mouth; meditate on it day and night, so that you may be careful to do everything written in it. Then you will be prosperous and successful" (Jos 1:8). "Blessed is the man...(whose) delight is in the law of the Lord, and on his law he meditates day and night" (Ps 1:1–2). "I open my mouth and pant, longing for your commands" (Ps 119:131). "When your words came, I ate them; they were my joy and my heart's delight" (Jer 15:16). "Now the Bereans were of more noble character than the Thessalonians, for they received the message with great eagerness and examined the Scriptures every day to see if what Paul said was true" (Acts 17:11).

Meditating...delighting...eating...panting...longing...eagerly examining. A disciple-making church has to create and sustain a culture in which people burn with passion to know and apply the Word.

Daily Immersion

To become like Jesus we must live the way that Jesus lived. To have a mind transformed by the Word we must immerse ourselves in the Word as Jesus did. When he says, "The one who holds to my teaching is truly my disciple" (Jn 8:31) we must agree that "holding to" his teaching is more than learning *about* it—obedience means making the instruction of Jesus an actual, daily part of life's routine. Transformation requires a plan to get started and perseverance to keep on track.

A good place to start is to set aside a specific portion of each day to read the Bible and simply to reflect upon it. There's no rush. This is not a race. Many disciples have identified the essential elements of such a time:

Stop
Ruthlessly carve out a 15–20-minute period of time to sit in the presence of God every day.
Mute
Hit the "off" button on your TV remote; welcome silence into your life instead of background noise.

Pray

Surrender your whole heart and mind to the work of God's Spirit, asking the Spirit to help you see the details of your life from God's perspective.

Read

Dig into the Bible a few paragraphs at a time.

Apply

Daily put into practice at least one thing you have learned; meditate or chew on a word, a phrase, or a verse.

This pattern of intentional personal engagement with the Word has been passed, life-to-life, for hundreds of spiritual generations: Barnabas to Paul, Paul to Timothy, Timothy to "faithful people who are able to teach others also" (2 Tm 2:2). Sustaining this pattern anchors our hope that the next spiritual generation will know Christ's liberating truth *firsthand*.

We don't have to resolve every issue, doubt, and question regarding the details of Scripture to go forward. Pascal was right: "The heart cannot believe what the mind knows to be untrue." Honest questions deserve honest answers. But we cannot permanently shift our spiritual life into "neutral" while awaiting satisfactory answers to every query. Christians of every age, while acknowledging the ever-changing menu of vexing questions, have agreed that we already have in hand sufficient reasons to trust God. Billy Graham once said, "A rocket that's always sitting on the launchpad being refueled never has to worry about guidance, because it's not going anywhere. But if that rocket is launched, its guidance system will click in, as designed." As we step out and put into practice what we're learning, even if we know merely the beginning of what God is calling us to do and to be, God has promised to transform our willingness into the renewing of our inner worlds.

At times the pace of that transformation may seem as slow as the creeping of tectonic plates. Then again, those plates *did* manage to push up the Rocky Mountains. God is faithful. As we bring our minds into alignment with the Word, we shall be changed.

Ever-Deepening Meanings

The maturing disciple ultimately arrives at a place where an academic approach to Scripture is supplanted by a far richer experience:

From: The Bible is something to be studied.

To: The Bible is something to be breathed.

How serious are you about knowing Chicago? If you're utterly serious, you won't just drop in for a visit every now and then. *Move there.* Become a resident. That's our call when it comes to God's Word. Why should we be tourists when we can live in these words and they can live in us for the rest of our lives? In particular we want to make sure that our Bible learning doesn't get stuck in our heads so that it never works its way out through our hearts and our hands. Notice in Joshua 1:8 that the essential purpose for his daily meditation was so that he might be "careful to do" whatever he had gleaned from the Word.

The further we move ahead as disciples, the more we discover that God speaks to us through the same text of Scripture in ever-deepening ways. Right after Joshua received the command to meditate on God's law he heard these words: "Have I not commanded you? Be strong and courageous. Do not be terrified; do not be discouraged. For the Lord your God is with you wherever you go."

Year by year, as we keep coming back to that verse, we discover new dimensions to the reality of God's being with us. Many things can happen between visits to Joshua 1:9. We may have broken up with someone we loved. Perhaps we lost the job we thought we would have forever. Maybe we've watched New York skyscrapers collapse. Now when we read once again that we do not need to be terrified or discouraged, we receive that news with an altogether different depth of gratitude and wonder. Only a mind transformed by the Word knows that all earthly terrors are groundless, and that no discouragement need ever be final. We can know the truth. And as Jesus said, it is that truth alone that sets us free.

A Fish Story

The tale is told of a young man who announced to his father that he was enrolling in theological studies at a particular seminary. His father, who had a serious regard for the authority of Scripture, had his doubts about this school. It was the kind of institution that might debunk the Bible's miracle stories. He said to his son, "I just hope that when you get back, the story of Jonah and the fish is still in your Bible."

Three years later, when the son had completed his studies, that's the very question the father asked him. "So, is Jonah still in your Bible?" "Gosh, Dad, why do you ask that? Jonah isn't even in *your* Bible." "Of course it is!" retorted his father. "Then show me," answered the son. For several minutes the father frantically scoured his Old Testament searching for Jonah. "It's not there, Dad," said his son. "The day I left for seminary I opened up your Bible and cut the book of Jonah out. Now tell me: *What's the difference between not believing that it's true, and paying so little attention to it that you don't even realize that it's gone?*"

That's the question that swirls around the second mark of a disciple. Are we willing to learn—*and to put into practice*—the very words of God? It takes a lifetime, but it can be done. And no endeavor is more worthy of our time.

The Bible's "Top Forty"

There is no such list, of course—but here are the "addresses" of forty of the Bible's best known chapters and stories.

1. Creation, Eden and the Fall (Genesis 1–3)
2. Noah and the Ark (Genesis 6–8)
3. Abraham and the Sacrifice of Isaac (Genesis 22)
4. The Story of Joseph and His Brothers (Genesis 37–45)
5. Moses in the Nile and at the Burning Bush (Exodus 1–4)
6. The Ten Plagues, Passover and Red Sea (Exodus 7–14)
7. The Ten Commandments (Exodus 20)
8. Joshua Confronts the Walls of Jericho (Joshua 1–6)
9. The Misadventures of Samson (Judges 13–16)
10. The Love Story of Ruth (Ruth 1–4)
11. David vs. Goliath (1 Samuel 17)
12. Job's Plight and God's Response (Job 1–3, 38–42)
13. The Shepherd Psalm (Psalm 23)
14. David's Personal Confession (Psalm 51)
15. Psalms of Worship and Praise (Psalms 93–100)
16. God's Intimate Love and Care (Psalm 139)
17. Soaring on Wings Like Eagles (Isaiah 40)
18. The Messiah as Suffering Servant (Isaiah 53)
19. The New Covenant is predicted (Jeremiah 31)
20. Three Men in the Oven (Daniel 3)
21. Daniel in the Lion's Den (Daniel 6)
22. The Story of Jonah the Reluctant Preacher (Jonah 1–4)
23. The Christmas Story (Matthew 1–2; Luke 1–2)
24. The Word Became Flesh in Jesus (John 1)
25. Jesus' Sermon on the Mount (Matthew 5–7)
26. Jesus Feeds 5000 and Walks on Water (Mark 4)
27. Jesus Talks to Nicodemus (John 3)
28. Parables of the Good Samaritan & Lost Son (Luke 10, 15)

29. Jesus' Prediction of the End of the World (Matthew 24)

30. Palm Sunday, Last Supper, Trial & Crucifixion (Mark 11–15)

31. Jesus Rises from the Dead (Luke 24, John 20)

32. The Holy Spirit Arrives on Pentecost (Acts 2)

33. Paul Meets Jesus on the Road to Damascus (Acts 9)

34. Nothing Can Separate Us From God's Love (Romans 8)

35. Love is the Greatest Quality (1 Corinthians 13)

36. The Fruit of the Holy Spirit (Galatians 5)

37. Rejoice in the Lord Always (Philippians 4)

38. The Hall of Fame of Faith (Hebrews 11)

39. Because God is Love, We Should Love Each Other (1 John 3–4)

40. Our Future in Heaven (Revelation 21–22)

Questions for Further Exploration

Personal, one-on-one, or small groups

1. Where would you place yourself in the "gaps" on this mark—as a seeker, a beginner, an intermediate, or a mature disciple?

2. "It is hard to live for Jesus." What, in your opinion, is the hardest thing about living for Jesus in today's world?

3. Have you ever had a season of voracious hunger for God's Word? What brought this about, and what was the outcome?

4. What is the cutting edge of Bible study right now in your church? What, in your opinion, is the need of the hour?

5. Can you think of a Bible text whose meaning has changed or grown a great deal in your own experience over the years?

Getting Started

On Your Own

The transformation of a mind through the study of God's Word cannot be accomplished via shortcuts. It will require time. Assess your current weekly allocations of minutes and hours to every major activity that is part of your routine. How much time every week are you presently committing to personal spiritual development and biblical study? How much time do you think God is calling you to commit? List the priorities and activities that will need to shift in order to fulfill that call—and sit down and share your plan of action with someone else.

As a Congregation

Every church is presented with the challenge of teaching its affiliates the basic storyline of the Bible. If your church has never identified the broad outline and main points of the Old and New Testaments, launch a team that will produce such a statement. This project may take a number of months. If your church has already identified the essential narrative of Scripture, investigate whether the major age groupings in your flock—children, teenagers, young adults, mid-lifers, and seniors—are hearing this message on a repeating basis, and whether they have "made it their own."

How do you plan to do the crucial step of evaluation?

10

ARMS OF LOVE

As the hands and feet of Jesus in the world, we
come alongside others in need, extend compassion,
welcome the stranger, and live in a community
of mutual care with other disciples.
We are on a journey of unconditional love.

*"By this all men will know that you are my
disciples, if you love one another."*

(John 13:35)

A few years back I found myself needing to kill five minutes
in the lobby of a coffee shop. My eyes were drawn to an
odd-looking machine, which in bright red letters posed
an intimidating question: "What Kind of Lover Are You?" Protruding
from the machine was a life-sized plastic hand. I read the instructions. If I deposited a quarter and squeezed the hand, this machine
would cause a little pointer to move, which would provide an immediate appraisal of the steaminess of my love life.

It occurred to me that since I shake many hands on Sunday morning, this might be useful information. I've often wondered if the people exiting our worship services think, "Now that was the handshake of a great lover." Looking up at the scale, I assumed I would probably register somewhere between *Torchy* and *Macho*.

The other end of the scale, however, looked less friendly. Depending on how I took hold of that plastic hand, I might end up somewhere between *Wimp* and *Mr. Freeze*. What was the machine looking for? Should I bear down hard, like a guy who makes anvils for a living, or should I take a more sensitive approach? In the end I did neither. I concluded it would be bad stewardship to spend twenty-five cents shaking hands with a machine in a coffee shop just to find out that I'm a wimp.

Our culture's obsession with love has clearly gotten out of hand—no pun intended. Songs, movies, clothing, fragrances, advertising, automobiles, and entire industries promise the delivery of intoxicating relationships. In the movie *The Princess Bride* the hero suffers a tragic death. But wait. He can be resurrected if he was in fact pursuing an ultimately worthy cause. "True love" is the mission that brings him back to life. In our society true love is the ultimate prize. If the Bible says God is love, America says love is God. It would be tragic to live and die without experiencing true love. How can we make sure we don't miss out?

How Do You Qualify for Love?

To that heartfelt question Western culture has developed, over the past 300 years, a cruel four-part answer. To experience real love you need to qualify according to at least one of the following parameters. First, *be beautiful*. This is about as frustrating as telling prospective basketball players, "Now make sure you grow really tall." No one has the luxury of self-selecting their chromosomes, and cultural concepts of beauty change every few years anyway.

So, try number two: *Be lovable*. Be the kind of person others want to be near. Unfortunately this generates a lifelong preoccupation with questions like, "How am I coming across? Am I clever? Am I gracious? Am I amusing?" Other people come to have enormous power over me—their opinions literally determine whether I'll be happy today.

Failing the standards of beauty and lovability, we can always attempt to *be alluring*. Where genetics and temperament fall short we can turn to chemistry, cosmetics, and color-coordinated accessories. Product lines promise to turn back the clock and open the blind eyes of potential partners. Recently I ran across an ad for a product called "Love's Bouquet" with the headline, "Never Be Lonely Again!" The ad read, "Just a touch or two of this powerful 'love-potion-in-a-bottle' is all you need to captivate a new partner or revive a flagging romance. Love's Bouquet contains a fiercely irresistible chemical formula which DRIVES the opposite sex to you without conscious awareness on their part. They can't help themselves. Age or appearance simply doesn't matter. Jennifer from Wisconsin says, 'Men who were shy are now genuinely unable to stay away from me.'" I found myself thinking: Is the answer to our church's search for deeper fellowship just a few drops of Love's Bouquet in the communion wine?

When all is said and done, the world's prescription for finding real love is the fourth one, *be lucky*. Love happens—but in the lottery of life, there's no guarantee that you'll be standing in the right place at the right time to receive it. What happens when we come to believe that the experience we crave the most—being loved—is bound up with physical beauty, social skills, or dumb luck? We end up living with a kind of desperation, investing heavily in shallow appearances, and frequently failing to develop the beauty of our real selves.

Love's Awesome Source

The church faces a monumental task. Our culture sings, *all we need is love*. Our call is to teach the world a new song. What we all need more than anything is a passionate devotion to Jesus Christ. Ironically, aiming for love almost guarantees that we will miss receiving it. Aiming at Jesus provides love as the most obvious benefit of that relationship. Discovering love's true origin is the primary "gap" that must be bridged for the spiritual seeker.

From: My search for love is limited to my own emotions, relationships, and personal experiences.

To: I know that God loves me unconditionally and gave his Son to die for me.

What we learn from Scripture is that real love is not about chemistry, and it's not about feelings. It is not a tidal wave of romantic sentiments that washes us helplessly from one experience to another. If there really is a potion that drives other people to our sides, against their wills, then we may be sure that what is driving them is not love. The Bible assures us real love doesn't come our way because we are pretty enough, clever enough, or *enough* of anything. We are loved because God loves us. Period. "Here's what love is—not that we loved God, but that he loved us" (I Jn 4:10).

What if we only had one description of love in the Bible, and it was what we read two sentences earlier, in I John 4:8? "Whoever does not love does not know God." If we fully took into account our consistent failure to love those around us, then we could safely conclude that none of us truly "knows God." We have to look still farther ahead in John's narrative, to verse 19: "We love because he first loved us." God is the source of all love in the universe. God doesn't love us because "we go first." God is the initiator. In fact, the verbal form in I John 4:8 is best translated, "Whoever does not *actively keep on choosing love...*" Our relationship with God—"knowing God"—is revealed by a consistent and ever-growing impulse to love others, even though we regularly fall short of that ideal.

The Meaning of Agape

The Greeks had a wide vocabulary for their experience of love, and the apostle Paul could have chosen any number of words to express one human being's care for another. But when it came time to declare the essence of God's love for us—and the kind of love that God commands us to *choose*—Paul reached for a word that was rarely used in Greek culture, perhaps because it was so rarely imagined that such a thing might be possible. Paul chose the word *agape*, which describes a love that has no condition or boundaries. Every time we see the word "love" in Paul's much-celebrated discussion of this subject in I Corinthians 13, we are seeing a rendering of the word *agape*.

What do we know about this extraordinary word? According to the Bible, *agape* comes from one and only one source in the universe. That source is God. If our hearts are filled with *agape*, it is only because God has placed it there. All of us are capable of receiving and carrying God's *agape* love, but it's equally true that all of us leak. We regularly need refillings. It's not as if we received all the love we would ever need back in 1989. *Agape* needs to be replenished every day. Filling our hearts with God's love is a little bit like traveling to Niagara Falls in order to fill a water bucket. There is no serious possibility that the water will run out before our buckets are full, no matter how many times we make that trip.

Furthermore we learn that God cannot be diminished by sharing his *agape* with us. "(Love) always protects, always trusts, always hopes, always perseveres. *Agape* never fails" (I Cor 13:7–8). Sometimes we humans are afraid to love. We've taken out our clipboards and meticulously made an internal inventory. We've measured exactly how much love we have in the reserve tank, and we know there's no way that there's enough to go around. God needs to stop sending new people into our lives, because we're afraid that if we love too many people too completely, we will be left completely empty.

Couples and intimate groups of friends may especially be prone to this concern. They are afraid to widen the circle of their affection for fear their love might get watered down. A husband and wife who are expecting a child sometimes shiver to think how this new baby might affect the balance of love at the center of their relationship. Parents who already have one child, whom they absolutely adore, cannot fathom sharing such love with a second child. We simply trip over the math. If we've been experiencing this much unconditional love, and the family is now growing from three to four, that means everybody is going to get 33 percent less love. The older child, of course, dreads the possibility of seeing his or her love gauge drop even by 1 percent.

What actually happens, however, in our own experience? We may worry about division, but *agape* is all about multiplication. When God is the source, there's always enough love to go around. There's always enough space to widen our circle of friends. Children who grow up with ten brothers and sisters frequently report that their house was the most loving home on the block.

Enthralled by the Love of God

Some of us tend to say at this point (although not loudly), "Thanks for the inspirational theology. But that's not what I'm hungry for. I crave the thrill of affection and the joy of security that happens only in intimate relationships." To which God responds, "Yes, I created you with that hunger—a hunger for love that is quenched only in relationship with me." Believers of previous generations have understood that intimacy with God is the end of the search for real love. Sixteenth century poet John Donne penned these striking verses of passion:

> *Batter my heart, three-personed God*
> *Take me to You, enthrall me, for I*
> *Unless You imprison me, shall not be free*
> *Nor chaste, unless You ravish me.*

The Bible declares that "true love" is being enthralled by the love of God. Knowing the love of God with our hearts and our minds is life's highest experience and its ultimate reward. And the best news is this: We don't have to be beautiful or lucky to receive what God gives for free. Jesus thus calls his disciples to extend arms of love in precisely the same way—proactively sharing what we have received from God with those around us. That's the gap that beginning disciples see stretching out before them.

From: God loves me.

To: God loves me unconditionally, so now I can and ought to love others unconditionally.

The Most Excellent Way

Twenty-three times in the New Testament we are commanded to love each other. Can feelings be commanded? Absolutely not. But behaviors can be commanded, and attitudes can be deliberately cultivated. In the Bible, love means seeking the good of other people even if we never have warm or positive feelings toward them. For many of us, that may include family members.

We don't love other people because they are attractive or lovable. We love them because God has poured his own love into our hearts. Paul says that agape is "the most excellent way" for us to be in relationship with other people (I Cor 12:31)—to seek their highest good, just as God seeks our highest good at every point.

Whatever situation you are facing right now, love is the right response. Love is the most excellent way, because love is God's only way. In the opening paragraph of I Corinthians 13, Paul holds up three tempting alternatives—supernatural gifts, superior insight, and supreme commitment. Three times he asks, "Is this what success looks like? Is this how someone can experience God's greatest treasures?" All three times he answers his own question by saying, "No! Love is more important than each of these. Love is the only way to go."

First he writes, in verse 1, that supernatural gifts are not the highest priority of the Christian life. "If I speak in the tongues of men and of angels, but have not love, I am only a resounding gong or a clanging cymbal." Paul makes his second point in verse 2: "If I have the gift of prophecy and can fathom all mysteries and all knowledge, and if I have a faith that can move mountains, but have not love, I am nothing." Superior insight may seem like an awesome thing. Without love, however, it turns us into spiritual zeroes.

Superior insight has never been God's way forward. In *The Letters to the Corinthians*, Bible commentator William Barclay wrote, "More people have been brought into the church by the kindness of real Christian love than by all the theological arguments in the world, and more people have been driven from the church by the hardness and ugliness of so-called Christianity than by all the doubts in the world" (Westminster John Knox Press, 1975).

Third, Paul says that supreme commitment ranks less than number one in God's pantheon of values. He writes in verse 3, "If I give all I possess to the poor and surrender my body to the flames, but have not love, I gain nothing." A culture of affluence would be impressed by someone willing to liquidate all of their assets and then write the biggest check that the local food bank has ever received. Or how about something more dramatic? Apparently Paul was acquainted with a monument in the city of Athens that memorialized a man who had burned himself alive as a way of demonstrating his absolute commitment to his beliefs. What outrageous thing might you do in the name of Jesus to earn sixty seconds of coverage on CNN this evening?

It's all meaningless, Paul says, unless we choose to love. The scandal of ABC Christianity in the United States is that we don't live as if we believe this. Surely God will be impressed with our baptismal statistics. The papers will take note when we break ground on the new wing. The youth director will get a raise because she doubled the number of students on this year's work camp. *But it is all less than nothing if it's not about agape from start to finish.*

What the world needs now is a church that has arms of love.

Love is as Love Does

The love that disciples share is not a feeling. Fifteen specific behaviors are itemized in verses 4 through 7 of I Corinthians 13. Such actions entail what it means to love. "Great lovers" aren't those who "can't stay away from each other." They are people who by God's grace learn to keep a lid on their anger…who are patient longer than they ever thought possible…who get excited about somebody else's big day…and who refuse to keep records of emotional hurts. The more we welcome God's love into our hearts, the more we possess the power to be hopeful. We look for signs of life in all our relationships and do our best to encourage them—refusing to set deadlines or timetables. Love never gives up because its source and its security is God, not the possible responses of other people. *Love is as love does.*

One Sunday morning we invited our congregation to provide written responses to this question: *Would you be willing to share an experience in which another member or friend of ZPC became a servant in your life—through an act of love, support, or simply a "random act of kindness"?* We received sixteen pages of personal accounts of kindnesses offered and kindnesses received.

171

The extraordinary moment came when we made these anonymous reports public. Far beyond mere preaching and theologizing, they compounded our church's vision for being the hands and feet of Jesus. Bear with me as I share a few of these messages here.

> As a single mother with no family here, a very kind, thoughtful single mom asked us to join her extended family for a Mother's Day lunch. I would have been alone again on a holiday. How much I appreciated the gesture.

> One Sunday the message was about God's grace and I had been deeply touched by it. Through the sermon tears had flowed down my face as I finally began to understand the blessings I'd been given, and that I needed to do more to serve God through those blessings. A woman walked up to me in the gathering space afterward and just gave me a hug. She simply said, "I just wanted to give you a hug." She was gone as quickly as she had come. I felt a part of this church. It was truly a blessing.

> When our son was born, church members provided more food than we could have ever eaten! Also, they provided fast food coupons (gift certificates) for my oh-so-picky husband! What a way to go out of their way to be sure we were all made to feel so special.

A number of people wrote about the power of receiving unexpected sacrifices:

> I thank God for someone who cut our grass all summer after my husband's heart attack...who decorated the outside of our house one Christmas when he was sick...who sent cards on "unofficial" occasions.

> During an extremely difficult time emotionally and physically, I became unable to care for my family in any way. At that time, several couples "adopted" my family: fed them, watched the kids, ran errands, anything that was needed.

During a time when I was feeling very low and lost and alone, a member stood by my side—brought dinner, sent notes, and set up a time to walk and talk with me—her encouragement through friendships, prayer, and listening showed me how generous God's love is.

Acts of love, more than anything else, regenerate lost hope:

The first Sunday I visited here, I was at a very low point in my life. In the message I heard that when we stand at an abyss we can either fall, or step back and consider our options. That day, I decided to try again, not to give in and give up.

I had the experience of teaching Sunday School. A young boy with a learning problem had trouble coloring. I made sure each Sunday I helped him. We have become great friends. His mother once told me, "If you ever wonder if you have made a difference in someone's life, you have." This is my greatest accomplishment to date.

On Christmas Eve afternoon a special person who attends ZPC surprised me with a phone call asking me to please join her and her extended family for the entire day of Christmas—breakfast through dinner. Thanks to that wonderful, special heart of that woman, I did not take my life. God shouted that he needed me.

Whenever we step forward in the name of Jesus with arms of love, *Jesus himself is stepping forward*. God is shouting, "I need you!" whenever his servants choose to bear that message. Our next challenge is to extend our circle of care beyond the opportunities that are convenient for us.

From: I unconditionally love in word and in action others who don't cost a lot to love.

To: Increasingly I unconditionally love in word and in action whomever God puts in my path.

Learning to Love Difficult People

Agape is the love that God has for each one of us, and it is the love that he commands that we willingly share with others—not if and when we feel like it (because we rarely will), and not because we see the wisdom in it (because quite frankly we will often think agape is downright foolish), but simply because God says, "This is how I live all the time, and I want you to be just like me."

Real love hangs in there—even with difficult people—even when circumstances compel others to walk away. We live in a nation that has come to assume that quitting is normal. We're used to hearing stories about pro athletes bailing on the team that invested in them because somebody else is offering a few more bucks; or the increasing number of people who RSVP to attend parties and weddings but then feel like doing something else when Saturday actually rolls around; or professional workers who will sign a commitment to finish a job, but then ignore the deadline. It doesn't seem surprising any more when people suddenly change churches, or start working for their former business competitor, or show up with a new marriage partner.

Agape, however, is that extraordinary quality of God's love that makes a promise and then keeps it, that starts down a worthy path and then stays on it, even when the emotions and the good intentions at the beginning of that journey have long since disappeared. What we're also going to find out is that every time we try to generate these behaviors on our own, we're in for a struggle. It's not that there are just a few people out there who are particularly difficult to love. *Every* human being is difficult to love, and not one of us is adept at delivering a God-like level of grace.

Infinite Value of Human Life

Disciples who extend arms of love to everyone, regardless of their

174

condition, are making a dramatic statement to our culture about the Creator's regard for every person. British scientist Richard Dawkins, an outspoken Darwinist, in his book *The Selfish Gene* wrote, "We are survival machines—robot vehicles blindly programmed to preserve the selfish molecules [of DNA] known as genes" (Oxford University Press, 1976, pp. 2–3). In other words, the only purpose of human life is DNA survival. A person is nothing more than DNA's way of making more DNA. Life is matter and only matter. Therefore, as persons, *we* do not matter.

When scientists publicly announce such "discoveries" as unchallengeable truth, it's not surprising that there are ramifications for society. It's not a shock that when people are declared to be machines, we start treating each other like machines. We begin to relate to each other as if we have no value. The frail, the weak, and the outcast are inevitably compromised. Gradually they are pushed away from life's table.

The biblical perspective is that every man and woman, as an image-bearer of God, has infinite value. We do not exist separately or independently, but are created to be in community with each other. We change others and we ourselves are changed by the wonder of being in relationships—relationships that are fueled and sustained by God's gift of *agape*.

Fresh Fillings of God's Love

Scripture also tells us that *agape* love cannot be faked—at least not for very long. Paul writes in I Corinthians 13:4, "Agape is patient, agape is kind. It does not envy, it does not boast, it is not proud." There's a world of difference between trying to look as if we are patient and kind, and actually *being* patient and kind because God's love has found a transforming home within our hearts.

The highway that runs alongside our church was subjected to a two-year construction project—a process that in retrospect seemed specially designed to shape my character. Once, during that project, I was in a bit of a hurry and accelerated toward a particular intersection to make sure I made the light. I found myself, however, behind a small red car whose driver seemed confused by the construction barricades. He slowed down, chose one lane, then another lane, and finally ended up straddling both available lanes—and I missed the light. I sat there in my car just burning. I mean, what a knuckle-head. Why couldn't he just move over and let me plough through? After the light turned green and he actually settled on a single lane, I let him know what I thought by racing by in a hurry. Immediately I thought, "What am I doing? Can't I extend grace even for half a minute? I sure hope nobody saw what just happened."

Two days later I got a voice mail from a church member. He said, "Glenn, you couldn't have known this, but the other day at 96th Street my wife and I were right behind you when you pulled up behind that red car. I just wanted to call and tell you something. We were so moved by how gracious and patient you were. I would have been going crazy. But the way you responded has been an example for my wife and me these past two days."

You know what? Sometimes it's possible to imitate the qualities of *agape* love without having the faintest bit of *agape* in our hearts. Sometimes we can even fool ourselves. But we cannot fool God. And the only way we will ever know the reality of God's love is by making a choice. Every day we must choose to receive a fresh filling of his *agape*, and to ask for the grace to learn how to love when love isn't easy.

Costly Love

The mature expression of the third mark of a disciple is one of life's greatest dramas. In a broken world, we may be sure that we will be challenged to close the following gap on a regular basis:

From: Increasingly, I unconditionally love in word and
         action whomever God puts in my path.

To: Because of Christ in me, I love others regardless of
         the cost.

Sometimes the cost is more than we can humanly fathom.

During the days following the September 11, 2001, terror at-
tacks, angry people demanded revenge. This is where "WWJD"
was suddenly elevated from a slogan on a bracelet to a very serious
question. *What would Jesus do?* In Matthew 5:38 Jesus said, "You
have heard that it was said, 'Eye for eye, and tooth for tooth.' But
I say to you, Do not resist an evil person. If someone strikes you
on the right cheek, turn to him the other also." Was Jesus teaching
that a nation should never respond to acts of evil?

Note the specific words Jesus chose for this crucial paragraph
of the Sermon on the Mount. "If someone strikes you on the right
cheek..." Right-handedness was assumed in the ancient world.
Moms and dads worked overtime to convert their natural southpaw
children into "righties." So how would a right-handed person strike
you on the right cheek? Would it be with a closed fist? No—it would
be a backhanded slap. Jesus' teaching in this paragraph addresses
the specific situation of a personal insult. How do we respond to
those who trash-talk us in public, to the coworkers who conspire
to intercept our praise and our promotions, to the neighbors who
would love to see us take a dive? We refuse to retaliate. Jesus says,
"Turn the other cheek." That is love in action, even when the cost
is high.

But that's not everything the Bible has to say about retaliation.
The apostle Paul writes in Chapter 13 of the book of Romans: "He
who rebels against...authority is rebelling against what God has insti-
tuted, and those who do so will bring judgment on themselves...For
rulers hold no terror for those who do right, but for those who do
wrong...(A ruling authority) is God's servant to do you good. But if

you do wrong, be afraid, for he does not bear the sword for nothing. He is God's servant, an agent of wrath to bring punishment on the wrongdoer" (Rom 13:2,4).

Governments are called by God—by means of judges, lawmakers, police and soldiers—to act on behalf of individuals and entire people groups who have been wronged. The state, as Paul puts it, "does not bear the sword for nothing." That leads to an agonizing question. Is it ever permissible for a Christian, by violent force, to take the life of another human being? It is—as long as that Christian is acting obediently as an agent of the state on a mission to carry out true justice. But never should that kind of power be wielded apart from deep sadness that such horrific actions sometimes become necessary in a fallen world. And never should a Christian be personally consumed by hatred or a desire for revenge.

Learning to Love Those Who Hurt Us

History teaches us that responding to evil with malice in our hearts inevitably generates far greater evil. This is why Jesus calls us to love our enemies.

The last six verses of Matthew chapter five represent one of Christianity's most recognizable teachings for those outside the faith, but perhaps its least popular teaching for those on the inside. We all know that Jesus commands us to love our neighbors. That is not much of a stretch. The logical corollary to loving neighbors is to hate our opponents, to resist our enemies, and to work for the defeat of destructive people. But Jesus says, "No, that's not the pathway to real life. Instead, love your enemies and pray for those who persecute you." Why? Because that's the way Jesus himself related to destructive people. Given the chance in the Garden of Gethsemane to call on legions of angels who would spring him from the clutches of the Pharisees and toast the Romans who would soon nail him to a cross, Jesus, incredibly, prayed for those who hated him. "Father, forgive them." He asks us to do the same.

Every religion on the planet informs us that it makes sense to love people who will love us back. In Matthew 5:43–48, Jesus says, "What's so impressive about that? Even drug dealers watch each other's backs. If you're going to be a member of my kingdom, your goodness will need to be radically different. You will need to stand out. You will need to be...like *me*."

Jesus alone can help us love our enemies. But where do we even start? This is where we can be fully grateful that the biblical notion of love is not fuzzy, abstract, beyond our access, or packaged in drippy emotions. Our love must involve both prayer and action. Both are true to the way that Jesus faced his enemies.

Jesus says, "Pray for those who persecute you, who make your life miserable" (Mt 5:44). It's accurate to say that we cannot hate someone whom we are regularly lifting up in prayer. Pray that the rawness of God's reality and God's grace will break into the lives of any person who is intent on hurting you. Pray for their families. Pray for their children—that the next generation will know the Prince of Peace, and therefore choose to make peace instead of war.

What actions should we take? By God's grace, we seek opportunities to bless those who have refused to bless us. We do what God does for all of us—we seek their highest good. Certainly there will be times that we'll find ourselves thinking, "This is nuts! Why should I pray that someone who has tried to hurt me should even have a shot at receiving God's grace, and then top it off with acts of kindness?" At that moment, however, we must listen for another voice, a quiet voice that will say, "This is what it means to live like my Son. This is what it means to be an authentic disciple." God, who is the watcher of human hearts, promises, "I will see what you do. I will cause these hard choices to make your heart grow, and to bring about healing that could never have happened otherwise."

The greatest blessing is reserved for those we may not even know. *The world will literally recognize Jesus' life within us as we pour out this kind of love to others* (Jn 13:35). All we need is love—yes! And the only way to be so filled is to receive it from the one who declared himself to *be* love.

Questions for Further Exploration

Personal, one-on-one, or small groups

1. Where would you place yourself in the "gaps" on this mark—as a seeker, a beginner, an intermediate, or a mature disciple?

2. If you were to ask ten non-members of your church to identify its reputation, what do you think they would say? Would "loving" being at or near the top of the list? Why or why not?

3. Have you had a powerful, personal experience of receiving God's love through other Christians?

4. What experience have you had of responding to God's call to love a difficult person? How did God provide, and what did you choose to do?

5. Would you say that your church is currently facing an enemy? How can your congregation choose to respond in love?

Getting Started

On Your Own

Identify one person in your life whom you find difficult to love. Recognizing that authentic love is not a feeling but an action, and is not a reflex but an act of the will:

A. Ask God to give you sufficient power to love this person.

B. Pray every day for one week that God will bless this person.

C. Take a course of action that will enhance this person's life (this could be a word of encouragement, a gift, a letter, etc.).

D. If possible, do something secret to bless this person—something that only you and God will know about. *Choose to keep your secret.*

As a Congregation

Ask your members to provide written responses to this question: "Would you be willing to share an experience in which another member or friend of this church became a servant in your life—through an act of love, support, or simply a random act of kindness?" Tally the responses. Preserve their anonymity. Share them with your congregation as a means of growing your vision for being the hands and feet of Jesus to each other.

KNEES FOR PRAYER

Our posture before God is one of continual dependence, trusting deeply that God is in charge of everything, conversing always about how his work is being accomplished in and through our lives.

"One day Jesus was praying in a certain place. When he finished, one of his disciples said to him, 'Lord, teach us to pray.'"

(Luke 11:1)

The practice of prayer is notable for two reasons. First, prayer is the only aspect of Christian spirituality that cuts cleanly across party and denominational lines. Christians routinely lob grenades into the camps of their brothers and sisters when it comes to church administration, the Holy Spirit, how exactly the cross of Jesus "works" to bring us salvation, millennial speculations, human sexuality, and virtually every other theological and sociological issue. What can we all agree upon, and routinely experience together? Christians of every persuasion can sit down and talk to God.

A Journey of Intimacy with God

Prayer is also notable because its practice—men and women actually choosing to enter and sustain a dialogue with the living God—is so seldom a part of the ABC church. The church that is preoccupied with external benchmarks of success doesn't have time for prayer. Prayer is not sufficiently productive. It is not measurable. The absence of prayer connotes the absence of a prevailing dependence on God.

By contrast the disciple-making church, which is committed above all else to the imitation of Jesus, models itself upon the pervasiveness of his prayer life. Jesus chose to spend time alone with his Father before he made major decisions and faced major challenges—before he chose the twelve disciples, before he encountered the devil in the wilderness, before he broke bread, and before he faced the cross. Jesus also spent time in prayer after sending out his disciples on a major mission trip, and *after* the major event of feeding the 5,000. His life was marked by rhythms of "asking for" that were followed by moments of "thanking for," in which he evidently recovered his spiritual strength and balance. Jesus' life was punctuated by both mornings (Mk 1:35) and evenings (Mk 6:45,46) that were set aside for solitude in God's presence.

Sometimes Jesus prayed with fervency. He never seems, however, to have been in a rush. His prayer was never perfunctory. He never hurried through a kind of devotional pattern so that he could move on to *real ministry*—to teaching and to healing and to performing miracles. In a real sense Jesus' ministry was spending time with the Father. None of the other events of his life would have happened (or at least happened as they did) apart from designated periods of solitude and reflection. Eugene Peterson suggests that church leaders have just two jobs—to pray and to teach other people how to pray. We are most available for the Spirit to work in and through our lives when the fourth mark of a disciple has become central in our personal experience.

The Power of a Few

I speak as one who has known the poverty of a prayerless life. For years I blundered ahead with well intentioned plans to build the kingdom while scarcely taking time to converse with the king. Church leadership actually diminished my practice of prayer. There were sermons to write and deacons to train and bills to pay and disciples to baptize and copy machines to repair, ad infinitum. When my rpm's would lessen from time to time I would feel a distinct dread—the certainty that I was trying to fashion a spiritual body apart from the reality of the Spirit, and the suspicion that I didn't even know how to pray. I always assumed that *somebody, somewhere* was talking to God. Surely somebody was praying while we tried to start a new church. I just hoped no one noticed that the pastor was running too fast to get on his knees.

As it turns out, I was correct. A number of somebodies were praying. God burdened a small group of lay people to pursue prayer as their primary way of depending on God. Their zeal astonished me. Several of them initiated the practice of walking the perimeter of our church property every Sunday morning, well before the crowds arrived. They chose to stand where our teachers would teach; they sat where those in worship would seek God. They prayed for the first-time guest, for the one whose marriage was dissolving, for the one seeking hope, for the oldest and the youngest, for the newcomers and the leaders.

Ultimately their example led to the proliferation of prayer groups and ministry teams throughout our congregation. After almost running over two of these extraordinary individuals in the pre-dawn darkness of a winter morning as they reflectively strolled our parking lot, I wondered what kind of "prayer steroids" they were taking—and where I might fill a prescription of my own.

Beyond Stained Glass Saints

Most of us discover that God's call to a life of sustained spiritual conversation is a process that takes us from a fresh vision to gaining some practical knowhow to an ever-maturing experience of prayer. We first discover for ourselves that prayer matters.

> *From*: My experience of God's desire for me to enjoy intimacy with him is insufficient for me to want to pursue him wholeheartedly.
>
> *To*: I've experienced enough of God to choose to pursue an intimate relationship with him.

A man named David Rice Atchison was President of the United States for one day and didn't even know it. According to the U.S. Constitution in the nineteenth century, if neither the President nor the Vice-President officially occupied the office of chief executive, the president pro tem of the Senate moved to the oval office. On March 4, 1849, President James Knox Polk's term had lapsed and the newly elected President, Zachary Taylor, couldn't yet be sworn in because it was Sunday. For one day David Rice Atchison was technically President of the United States —something he didn't realize until he got to thinking about things a few months later.

When Christians get to thinking about things—specifically, when we are confronted by the teaching of Scripture—it should dawn on us that we hold a position of the highest honor and privilege. We are children of God. We have unrestricted access to our Father in heaven. We do not need to beg, plead, cajole or manipulate God into giving us the time of day. The challenge for spiritual seekers is to believe that such intimacy is genuinely available for less-than-whole people.

I grew up in a church surrounded by stained glass saints. Our sanctuary windows featured dozens of them—monumental, brightly colored portraits of men and women whose lives were right with God. Their faces were placid and trusting. Their heads were enveloped by golden auras or haloes. All of them were heroes of the faith. I don't ever remember thinking that I could be one of them. I don't remember a moment in which I even wanted to be like them. How could an ordinary person be a stained glass saint?

I was dimly aware of a need to pray. I wondered how God put up with my meandering attempts at trying to generate a conversation with him. I didn't know what to do with my body. Was I supposed to look somewhere? Should I close my eyes? Was I supposed to stand, or sit, or bow, or walk? Did I need to learn an entirely new vocabulary?

Three ministers once got together in a church study to discuss prayer techniques. In an adjoining room there happened to be a telephone repairman who was working on the lines. The first pastor said, "When I pray, I find it helps to hold my hands together like this, as a personal expression of worship." The second suggested that real prayer ought to be conducted on one's knees. The third pastor corrected him, saying, "The most biblically authentic posture for talking to God is to lie stretched out on one's face."

At that moment the telephone repairman, who'd been eavesdropping, poked his head around the corner and said, "I'd have to say the best prayer I ever prayed was when I was dangling upsidedown by my heels from a power pole about forty feet above the ground." What I didn't know all those years when I was staring at the stained glass saints is that most of them talked to God more like the telephone guy than those pastors. It had never occurred to me that in the Bible the Big Names regularly found themselves overwhelmed by Deep Anxiety.

Praying As We Can, Not As We Can't

In I Kings 19 Elijah cried out, essentially, "I have had enough, Lord. I'm the only one left who really cares about you, I've done everything that you asked me, and what do I get for my trouble? Right now there's a posse out hunting for my head." I didn't know that prayer could be fueled by such passion and despair.

Jeremiah moaned, "Since my people are crushed, I am crushed. I mourn, and horror grips me. Is there no balm in Gilead? Is there no physician there? Why then is there no healing for the wound of my people? Oh, that my head were a spring of water, and my eyes a fountain of tears!" (Jer 8:21–9:1). Gradually I learned that 70 percent of the Old Testament psalms could be construed as laments. God's people could pray from their guts. They could raise their voices, shake their fists, reveal their doubts, shed real tears, and shout for joy all within a few sentences.

It is immensely freeing to grasp that we can pray from weakness instead of strength. All it takes for a 911 operator to locate a person in need is for someone to pick up the phone and dial. A stroke victim need not talk. A sobbing person need not speak coherent words. The operator already knows a name and an address. We may be certain that the Holy Spirit knows much more about us every time we turn our broken hearts to the Lord. *Our prayers, whatever form they take, matter to God.*

Barriers to Prayer

The disciple who is just beginning to pray also has to ascend the "how to" learning curve:

From: My prayer life is awkward because I don't know how to talk with God.

To: I'm sufficiently experienced at prayer that I increasingly engage God in conversation.

Commentators have noted that on the pages of the four Gospels, Jesus' disciples only once asked him for specific instruction. They didn't ask, "Lord, teach us how to preach," or "Teach us how to baptize," or "Teach us a creative new approach to next year's stewardship campaign." They said, "Lord, teach us how to pray." As imitators of their rabbi, they asked for direction concerning a practice that was obviously and visibly an essential feature of his life.

At one juncture we surveyed almost five hundred members of our church concerning their personal experiences of prayer. We asked if they scheduled specific prayer times, and if they were satisfied with their own communication with God. We asked what was most helpful in forming their prayer lives. Our survey yielded seventeen pages of comments brimming with joys, insights, concerns, and hopes.

The majority of those who participated ventured that prayer is crucially important, but believed that they didn't pray often enough or effectively enough. Most voted enthusiastically for more prayer in our worship services, not less. At a time when we were pondering a noisier, more celebratory approach to worship, our own members steered us in a different direction. They begged for extended periods of silence—the very thing almost universally missing in their daily experience of God.

We asked, "What barriers do you experience when you pray?" There were hundreds of responses. Here's a smattering: "No time. Distractions. Hectic schedule. I don't feel I'm worthy to ask God for things I need through prayer. Time. Forgetfulness. My mind wanders. Too many other *have to's*. Poor management. I'm not sure I hear anything back. I just don't make the time."

Aspiring disciples seeking deeper experiences of prayer are often frustrated to discover that there is no book or method that suddenly removes those barriers. There is no seminar or program that finally clears away the fog. We must never trust our hearts to the ten-step plan to achieve "prayer that gets results." God is a person. God is approached and engaged person to person. Prayer is intelligent conversation about matters of mutual concern. Prayer is talking to God about what he and his people are endeavoring to accomplish together. The greatest leaps forward in our prayer lives always follow fresh glimpses of who God really is, and a growing trust that we *already* occupy privileged places in God's plan.

No Bad Prayers

Such trust will always be a hybrid trust—an awkward mixture of conviction and doubt, strength and weakness. Should we first try to attain more spiritual growth before we start to pray? Such a strategy is likely to lock us into an endless holding pattern; we will never pray—for we will never be as we should be.

The alternative is to pray as *we really are*, trusting that God is big enough to receive us with our mixed motives and our wounded spirits. In *Prayer*, Richard Foster writes about the "notion—almost universal among us modern high achievers—that we have to have everything 'just right' in order to pray" (HarperSanFrancisco, 1992, p. 7). Instead, from the Bible we learn that we don't have to pretend that somehow we have our acts together. We must pray as we can, not as we can't. We are ordinary people bringing ordinary concerns to an extraordinary God.

"Lord, teach us to pray." Jesus responded by saying that style points don't count. Disciples don't need to get hung up on technique. Jesus warned, "And when you pray, do not keep on babbling like pagans, for they think they will be heard because of their many words. Do not be like them, for your Father knows what you need before you ask him" (Mt 6:7). Those who don't know God or understand his ways try to leverage him by lengthening their requests, by piling on divine adjectives, or by praying in such a way that observers are impressed.

Jesus countered with a model prayer that is stark in its simplicity and astounding for its brevity. "When you pray, pray like this," he said, and then outlined a pattern of making six requests—three prayers that God's reign might extend over every part of the universe, and three prayers for God's ongoing personal provision. There are no "deep secrets" regarding the content of prayer. Obsession with polish and sophistication puts us in danger of missing the very point of baring our souls before God.

Every year we hang on our Christmas tree ornaments that our kids made when they barely knew how to color within the lines. Nowadays our children could do infinitely better. Does that mean we should abandon their first artistic efforts? Speaking as a father, none of my kids ever came home and said, "Here, Daddy," and then handed me a bad ornament. It's impossible for us to come to our heavenly Father and pray a bad prayer. All that God wants is for us to set before him what is *actually in us right now*—not what we think *ought* to be in us—even though someday, by God's grace, we may be able to make a greater offering of ourselves.

What if our prayers keep getting interrupted by other thoughts? What if we try to talk to God and our minds drift immediately to someone who owes us money, or to that touchdown that was called back by a penalty, or to lurid images, or to the person we've never been able to forgive? God is a very big God. He can handle what's really inside us. Ultimately, as we persist in simply and prayerfully presenting the ordinary details of our lives to God, there will come about what Foster calls a Copernican revolution in our hearts—the discovery that God isn't so much a part of our lives, as we are a part of his life (HarperSanFrancisco, 1992, p. 15).

A New Response to Reality

Paul infers in Romans 1:21 that the first and primary word that we speak to God is "thank you." Christian spirituality begins with heartfelt thanks for the finished work of Christ on our behalf. *Asking* God to meet specific needs, in all of their variety and complexity, requires another step forward.

From: My prayer life tends to be one-dimensional and inconsistent.

To: Through a more consistent prayer life, I am increasingly more open with God about all of my concerns.

Why is it that, for some of us, prayer is like the door at the side of the movie theater that says, "For Emergency Use Only"? The answer is that we have been schooled to believe that prayer is an occasional behavior instead of a pervasive lifestyle. Over the years, faced with the difficulties and the distractions of countless ordinary days, a good many of us have trained ourselves to respond in predictable, self-dependent ways. As soon as circumstances go out of our control—which turns out to be, if we really faced the truth, every minute of every day—our emotional reflex is to worry. Then we look for ways to interject occasional prayers against the background noise or "ground clutter" of almost unrelenting anxiety.

Paul proposed a complete makeover in the way we respond to reality. Prayer lies at the center: "Rejoice in the Lord always. I will say it again, Rejoice! Let your gentleness be evident to all. The Lord is near. Do not be anxious about anything, but in everything by prayer and petition, with thanksgiving, present your requests to God. And the peace of God, which transcends all understanding, will guard your hearts and your minds in Christ Jesus" (Phil 4:4–7).

We cannot negotiate our responses to difficult circumstances. We cannot say that the situation we're facing right now is so dismal that we're perfectly justified in throwing a hissy fit, or embracing a nervous breakdown, or in writing God completely out of the picture. According to Paul, there are no such situations. We cannot choose what happens to us, but we are spiritually empowered to respond wisely, no matter what.

Faced with any given situation, we can despair or rejoice. Existentialist philosopher Albert Camus suggested that the question most worthy of our attention is whether or not we should commit suicide. Camus refused to identify any unshakeable ground for personal hope. What about Paul? Note that he didn't say, "Rejoice always." That would be recommending an ungrounded commitment to positive thinking—like driving past an intensive care unit or a cemetery and smiling, "That's never going to happen to me." All kinds of difficult circumstances are indeed going to happen to us. Thus Paul says, "Rejoice *in the Lord* always." Our call is to access, by prayer, a deep personal gladness that whatever we're facing right now cannot separate us from God. Our hope isn't circumstantial. Our hope is connected to being in a relationship with an awesome God who cares for us.

This Moment Counts

Paul appeared to anticipate our sighs of skepticism. "Rejoice in the Lord *always*? Well, you're not in my situation. You have no clue how hard this is." Which is perhaps why Paul wrote, "Just so there's no question, let me say it again: Rejoice!" Paul, after all, was personally acquainted with hopeless situations. He wrote to the Philippians from Roman imprisonment with little expectation that he would ever be a free man again.

The hardest part, of course, is the word "always." Over the years I have tended to approach certain times and seasons with a grim attitude of survival. "My only value right now, my only goal, is to get through this weekend. Then things will get better." Sometimes I communicate that to my wife. "I know I'm busy and distracted today, but wait until Monday. Starting next Monday, I'll be free. This will all be over. I just need to slog my way through the tunnel of darkness from here to there."

What my wife knows from experience is that there's always another tunnel of darkness waiting on the other side. What I am learning is how seldom I rejoice in the midst of busy, frantic times. I may picture myself rejoicing at the finish line. But by doing that I have cut myself off from this moment—this irretrievable, irreplaceable moment—in which I can rejoice right now *in the Lord*. By doing so I am affirming, quite apart from my emotions, the reality of God's provision. Paul says, "Be alive now. Stop picturing life as tunnels of darkness. Joyfully connect during this moment with the God who is near" (or, as Paul put it, "at hand").

We can't push our lives forward and we can't go backward. Do we really want to live the rest of our lives wishing that this moment were some other moment than this moment? God is exclusively available to us in the present tense. What makes *this moment* count forever is that what we experience now has the power to transform all our future moments as well.

Who's in Charge?

Whatever situation we are facing, we can either worry or we can pray. When all is said and done those are life's two great alternatives. Either *we* are in charge—which means we have a whole lot of worrying to do—or *God* is in charge, which immediately transforms prayer from an every-now-and-then religious activity into an ongoing dialogue with the Great King.

Worry is conversation that I have with myself: "What am I going to do?" Prayer is conversation that I have with God: "God, please help me do what you would have me do."

Prayer doesn't force God's presence. Prayer doesn't *make* God materialize. The Lord is already and eternally at hand. Talking with God is our acknowledgment that God is near, and that God can be trusted.

Our titanic struggles of worry vs. prayer are generally settled within the first three minutes of any given day. Before we put on our socks, before we start the car, before we step into our very first appointment, we have a choice to make. We can pray, "Lord, this day belongs to you. I don't know precisely where the road is taking me. But I am glad that you have gone before me, and that you will always be walking beside me." Unless we fill our minds and put on our lips that kind of prayerful surrender, worry will be more than willing to rush in and fill the void. Worry will seize whatever ground we refuse to claim for God.

The best news is that a lifestyle of prayer unmasks our worries for what they really are—impostors. Scientists have run the numbers and concluded that a thick bank of fog that is 100 feet high and seven blocks square is comprised of less than one glassful of water. All the problems that we see before us, all the anxieties churning within us, are in the end as insubstantial as a mist compared to the reality of God's care.

The Courage to Ask

Paul wrote, "In everything, by prayer and petition...present your requests to God" (Phil 4:6). The call of God is that we actually ask for the experience of his presence, his provision, and his empowerment.

Every spring I have the privilege of joining about forty other congregational leaders for three days in a covenant group experience of prayer and sharing. A few years ago the airline I flew required me to switch planes in Raleigh, North Carolina. I had at least ninety minutes before my next flight, so I walked down to the departure gate just to make sure things were in order.

That's when I saw the sign. At the check-in counter there was a prominent notice that said, "Ask about our upgrades to first class." I thought, *Wow. That would sure be nice.* I grabbed a bite to eat, read a few pages from a book, then came back about forty-five minutes later. There sat Steve, one of the other pastors in my prayer covenant group, who had also been routed to this very gate. After we talked for a few minutes Steve said, "Hey, guess what? I'm flying first class the rest of the way—for free."

"You're kidding!" I said. "How did you pull that off?" "Well," said Steve. "Do you see that sign over there—the one that says, 'Ask about our upgrades to first class'? I asked. I just got the last seat available." Now I want you to know that I was truly happy for my friend Steve, who is six-feet, four-inches tall. But as I shoehorned myself into my spacious and elegant 737 coach seat and looked around and noticed that every single seat in our section of the plane was occupied, I had to wonder: Why didn't any of these people ask about the upgrade to first class? For that matter, why didn't *I* ask?

To tell you the truth, I think I assumed that the sign just had to be for somebody else. How nice it was to be flying with an airline that upgrades people as an act of grace. But I chose not to ask. That grace couldn't be for me. How tragic it would be to go through life knowing that a God of grace rules this world—but to be convinced that his richest gifts are reserved for other people. Honor God today: *Ask for the fullest possible experience of his gifts*.

Not My Will, but Yours

I can make no claim to having a "mature" experience of prayer. That is still a distant country for me. But it is a country that at long last I am able to imagine, and even to glimpse from time to time:

From: Through a more consistent prayer life, I am
         increasingly more open with God.

To: Prayer permeates my life and my soul and God is
         never outside my awareness.

Through the centuries, lifelong learners of Jesus have subjected one of his prayer experiences to the greatest scrutiny and reflection.

Huddled with his disciples in the Garden of Gethsemane just hours before his arrest, Jesus groaned, "My soul is overwhelmed with sorrow to the point of death." Mark tells us that "he fell to the ground and prayed that if possible the hour might pass from him. '*Abba*, Father,' he said, 'everything is possible for you. Take this cup from me. Yet not what I will, but what you will'" (Mk 14:34–36).

Being able to imitate this behavior is the ultimate challenge for anyone who aspires to the fourth mark of the disciple. God is Father. He is our intimate and adoring *Abba*. Everything is possible for this Father. *But not everything that we want is what the Father wants.*

Jesus presented himself to God, body and soul. With utter trust in the goodness of the Father, Jesus beseeched: *Don't make me go through this*. With the same utter trust in the goodness of the Father, Jesus relinquished his own agenda: *I will do whatever you want me to do*. Two wills: It was Jesus' will to shrink from this pain, and it was Jesus' will to do the will of his Father. He yielded the former so that he might fully experience the latter. This is spiritual mystery of the highest order.

Prayer is not about fulfilling our wish lists. Prayer is about joining our hearts with the heart of God. As we come into the presence of the Father, he asks us to do what Jesus did. *He asks us to die.* Unless we release our vise-like grip on our dreams, our desires, our affections, and our ambitions—the entirety of the way that we organize our lives apart from God's desires for us—the will of the Father, Son, and Holy Spirit cannot be fulfilled within us.

It has always been this way with God. Death precedes resurrection. Grain must be ground into flour before it becomes bread, and grapes must be crushed to release their juice. We belong most fully to the one we call Lord only when he has permission to crush those parts of us that we have tried the hardest to keep under wraps. This means that an ever-maturing expression of prayer is less and less about my requests of God, and more and more about God's requests for me.

I once heard a pastor describe his experience as a first-time skydiver. He had received parachute training, donned a jump suit, flown aloft, and witnessed other jumpers land safely on the ground. Poised at the open door of the aircraft he patted his parachute and asked his flight instructor one final question: "Is this thing really going to work?" His instructor smiled and said, "There's only one way to find out."

Can God be trusted—*in everything*? There's only one way to find out. Knees for prayer bring us face to face with the one who promises that in life and in death we have no greater security than his presence.

Questions for Further Exploration

Personal, one-on-one, or small groups

1. Where would you place yourself in the "gaps" on this mark—as a seeker, a beginner, an intermediate, or a mature disciple?

2. Who has been your model or your hero when it comes to prayer?

3. What has been your greatest personal obstacle in sustaining a life of prayer?

4. Where would you like to be in your prayer life one year from now? Five years from now?

5. Identify a time in which it was difficult for you to rejoice in the midst of your circumstances. How did God provide for you? Where, ultimately, did you see God at work in your life during this time?

Getting Started

On Your Own

Many disciples have found that keeping a prayer journal has been immensely helpful in sustaining their walk with God. Such journals may take many forms. Experiment with your prayer life over the next seven days by following a pattern like the one below:

A. Obtain a small notebook (some may choose a word processor).

B. Identify 10–12 individuals and/or concerns that you will bring to God in prayer every day for at least a week. Include an "enemy" or two. Include a particular city, country, or group that God seems to have laid upon your heart.

C. Set aside at least fifteen minutes each day for prayer and journaling. Ask the Holy Spirit to speak to you during this time. After praying through your list, re cord any thoughts you have. What new insights or discoveries are you making? What actions are you being led to take?

D. Consider such a prayer journal as a long-term part of your walk with God. As God leads you, revise your prayer list weekly, monthly, or annually.

As a Congregation

Resolve that you will no longer put up with perfunctory, same-as-always, "because we're supposed to" prayers at the beginning of meetings. Put as much thought into the opening time of prayer and reflection as the formation of the agenda. Consider identifying several non-clergy prayer or devotional champions for each major board or group in the church—individuals who will model new ways of bringing participants more authentically into the presence of God. Insist that this become a practice of all your church's leaders.

12

A VOICE TO SPEAK THE GOOD NEWS

We embrace the call to share Jesus with those who
do not know him, addressing the deepest questions
of both heart and mind, voicing hope and encouragement for people everywhere.

*"Always be prepared to give an answer to everyone
who asks you to give the reason for the hope that
you have. But do this with gentleness and respect."*

(I Peter 3:15)

Have you ever been on an elevator at a nice hotel or con-
ference center and noticed that there are people riding
alongside you who aren't actually going anywhere?
They're riding recreationally. Who are these people? Well, that would
be the McDonald family—at least, my children and I. Throughout
their early years we regularly took trips to the more sensational
elevators in our metro area, investing an hour or so doing nothing
more than exiting on various floors and watching others go up and
down.

Our favorite elevators by far are the ones at the local Hyatt. They are glass enclosures and look out over a vast atrium. One day I had three children in tow, all of them quite small at the time. The elevator we were riding in stopped suddenly at the seventeenth floor. At that moment my oldest son and I got our signals crossed. Just as several hotel guests walked on, Mark walked off. Before we could even speak to each other the door closed and the elevator descended. My young son was left behind, all alone on the seventeenth floor of a downtown hotel.

I looked at the child I was holding with my left hand and the child I was holding my with right hand and I thought, *Hey, at least I've got two-thirds of the kids I came with. That's not bad for a family trip.*

That's not exactly what I was thinking.

It's difficult to describe the rush of adrenaline and panic and terror and energy that you never thought lurked inside you, all focused into one unrelenting mission: *I've got to find the one who is lost.* I never compromised my commitment to the two children I had in hand in order to pursue the one. In fact I held onto them so tightly that one of them said, "Daddy, you're squeezing me." When at last we rendezvoused with Mark there was a major celebration.

From time to time we are briefly allowed to experience the pounding emotions that fill the heart of God at every hour. God has an unyielding passion to pursue and to lead to safety the one who is not at home, who is not secure, who is spiritually adrift. Whoever would be like Jesus must therefore ask, "Am I willing to join God in the pursuit of the one? Will I raise my voice to speak the good news that will help direct a lost person into the arms of God?"

A Journey Beyond Ourselves

It is alarming to consider the feeble response of America's Christians to those two questions. Social researcher George Barna (*Rechurch-*

202

ing the Unchurched, Issachar Resources, 2000), indicates that among the aggregate body of unchurched adults in the United States, 4 percent had been invited by a friend to attend church within the previous twelve months, and had done so; 23 percent were invited to attend, but declined; and 73 percent had not been invited.

Barna asks, "What does this tell us? Perhaps the most obvious observation is that most unchurched people are not being pursued by anyone. We outnumber them two to one. We are called by God to pursue them. We spend more than $3 billion every year in America constructing or renovating church facilities in which to host them. But the single most effective strategy of all—following Jesus...asking them to "come and see"—is generally neglected" (p.111).

Why, at the beginning of the twenty-first century, is the fifth mark of a disciple so challenging? It may be that American Christians are so thoroughly "of the world" that we only dimly see a distinction between ourselves and those outside the church. It may be that the multicultural, buffet-style approach to truth typical of our age makes it exceedingly uncomfortable to take a stand on spiritual issues. It may be that the basic skill set of describing our need of God and showing a seeker how to respond is a lost art in the Christian community. Or it may be (and I fear this is all too true) the average Christian has experienced so little of God himself that he has no idea there is good news worth sharing.

Methods, media, and marketing are not the need of the hour in order to voice the good news. Those who live apart from Christ are eager to see something else—to see the presence and the power of God at work *within us*, to experience the pounding heart of God's love through our love. The world is drawn by the radical invitation of One who asks for nothing less than everything, carried on the lips and embodied in the actions of disciples whose lives are proof that this Master can be trusted above all.

Casual Christians will most assuredly not transform this world for Christ. Jesus didn't flinch from saying that we are his only planetary strategy. There is no Plan B. So where do we begin?

Anxiety About the "E" Word

Young Christians are frequently touted as the church's first line of offense. The contagious enthusiasm of many new believers is embodied by a major shift of attitude with regard to faith-sharing:

From: I haven't yet experienced Jesus in such a way that I'm willing to respond to this call.

To: In response to what Jesus has done for me, I am willing to tell others about him.

In a postmodern climate, however, this shift cannot be assumed. It is increasingly likely that those who enroll as followers of Jesus will retain a high degree of respect for the convictions of non-Christians, and an accompanying suspicion regarding anything that resembles proselytizing. Rule number one of post-modernity is that you have your truth and I have mine, and claims for the superiority of one truth-version at the expense of another (that is, evangelism) is highly offensive.

In the cartoon world of *The Simpsons*, Homer and his dysfunctional brood live next door to the Flanders family, the neighborhood churchgoers. In one episode the Flanders kids arrive home from a trip: "We've been to church camp, to learn how to be more judgmental." That, in a nutshell, is mainstream America's perception of the church—a place where decent people are turned into religious people, which makes them truly scary to have as neighbors. Jay Leno held up a real-life "headline" in which a brothel complained that a church "would be bad for the neighborhood." Whereas churches used to be considered assets for any part of a metro area, zoning boards are increasingly saying "no" to new church developments, citing noise, traffic, and safety issues. What usually goes unspoken is the implied threat of evangelism.

The long and the short is that more and more Americans see the arrival of a church as a subtraction instead of an addition to their community. Fewer people want to live near an enclave of religiously convinced men and women.

Jesus and Religious People

First-time readers of the gospels are frequently surprised to learn that Jesus was put off by religious people, too. He consistently went out of his way to offend them. One would think that religiously zealous people would be Jesus' natural allies. Not so—as long as we are defining "religious people" as those whose first priority is the maintenance of good order and the keeping of ecclesiastical rules. The most important rule, of course, is that good people need to be rewarded and bad people need to be penalized. Religious people play by the rules, and they appreciate it when justice is served. The last thing they want (in the first century or in the twenty-first century) is for someone to come along and change the rules. But that's what Jesus did.

"Jesus _____s sinners." How should we fill in the blank? Religious people have a ready answer: "Jesus *condemns* sinners." At least that's what the answer ought to be. Jesus needs to take a stand and come down hard on people who cheat on their spouses, or get divorced, or do drugs, or abuse their kids, or cheat on their taxes.

What did Jesus himself say? The fifteenth chapter of Luke begins, "Now the tax collectors and 'sinners' were all gathering around to hear him (Jesus). But the Pharisees and the teachers of the law muttered, 'This man welcomes sinners and eats with them.'" Jesus *welcomes* sinners. That's what belongs in the blank. Not only that, Jesus eats *with* spiritually bankrupt people. In the Middle East to share a meal with someone is virtually a sacramental act signifying total acceptance. We can imagine what the religious people thought of *that*. Where are God's high standards? Why doesn't Jesus shun sinful men and women?

Insiders and Outsiders

Every congregation has to decide where to come down on this issue. Who do we think has the right perspective—religious people or Jesus of Nazareth? Is the local church ideally a holy huddle, inwardly focused on those who are already here? Or should every congregation focus outwardly on extending God's love to those who quite frankly don't appear to deserve an ounce of grace? In Luke 15 Jesus says, "Let me tell you what's on God's heart." He proceeds to tell three stories: one about a lost sheep, one about a lost coin, and one about a lost son. Our current purpose will be served by focusing on the first story.

Suppose one of you has a hundred sheep and loses one of them. Does he not leave the ninety-nine in the open country and go after the lost sheep until he finds it? And when he finds it, he joyfully puts it on his shoulders and goes home. Then he calls his friends and neighbors together and says, "Rejoice with me; I have found my lost sheep." I tell you that in the same way there will be more rejoicing in heaven over one sinner who repents than over ninety-nine righteous persons who do not need to repent" (Lk 15:4–7).

Notice how Jesus began: "Suppose one of you has a hundred sheep and loses one of them." Jesus clearly intended that we put ourselves into this story. We must assume the role of the shepherd. What exactly would a good and faithful shepherd do? Kenneth Bailey, in his insightful study of this parable, entitled *The Cross and the Prodigal*, declares that a good shepherd accepts responsibility for the loss (Concordia, 1973, pp. 21–22).

Bailey suggests that the Pharisees would have expected a different question: "Which of you, owning a hundred sheep, if a report came to you that one was lost, would not send a servant to the shepherd responsible and threaten him with a heavy fine if he didn't find the sheep?" Something is lost, so somebody has to pay. But Jesus says, "No, think again. *You* are responsible. *You* own a hundred sheep and *you* lost one of them."

It's intriguing that in the Middle East—both in Jesus' time and today—it is culturally inappropriate to accept blame. One would never say, "I'm late." The more typical answer is, "The rest of you went ahead without me." Instead of admitting, "I wrecked the wagon," one might announce, "There was an accident." But Jesus deliberately started this parable by saying, "None of you gets off the hook like that. You're a shepherd and you're responsible for some sheep and *you lost one of them*. Now...what are you going to do about it?"

We cannot say, "I live in postmodern times and evangelism is passé. It would be inappropriate for me to risk my relationships with my neighbors by talking about the One to whom I have given complete say-so in my life." Many of our neighbors are lost when it comes to the things of God. *They are lost.* If the answer to the question, "Who is your Lord?" is Jesus Christ, then you must accept the responsibility of putting on your heart what is most on his heart. We must share his pursuit of the one.

Not Transactions, but Relationships

Many long-time churchgoers are frozen in the "beginner" category of the fifth mark. They realized a long time ago that they are not going to step into the shoes of Billy Graham. That's a wise discovery. God's call is not that any of us tell Billy Graham's story, but that we learn to put into words how God has transformed our own story.

From: I'm not too knowledgeable about speaking the good news.

To: I can clearly articulate my own spiritual story and the story of Jesus.

Storytelling is the relational currency of postmodernity. For more than a century, however, the evangelistic efforts espoused by most American churches have been transactional. I proclaim the message of Jesus to a non-Christian. It is now his or her responsibility to listen, to ask questions, to wrestle with doubts or fears, and ultimately to capitulate. A prayer is prayed and a soul is "won" for Christ. That completes the evangelistic transaction. Another decision for the Lord can now be registered.

The call of Jesus, however, is that we make *disciples*, not *decisions*. Millions of people have responded positively to our spiritual invitations, but gone no further. This has been especially true when the very concept of "further" has been omitted from the transaction. Research demonstrates that numerous men and women have been ecclesiastically "counted" many times over, but have never enrolled as lifelong learners of Jesus.

Evangelism, as an organic component of the entire disciple-making task, cannot be squeezed into a transactional box. Bringing others to trust in Christ is relational. From beginning to end, becoming like Jesus is fundamentally accomplished by being in the right relationships. This is very good news indeed for Christ-followers in the twenty-first century. Storytelling is done best within trusting relationships, and our relationally hungry culture has open ears to hear how the story of Jesus has somehow become interwoven with our own.

That also makes this a strategic time to release our perception of evangelism as military conquest. Yes, there are some fine hymns about claiming occupied territory for our Leader. But rather than identifying themselves as targets for our spiritual cruise missiles, younger generations are more receptive to some of the alternative evangelistic metaphors that appear in the New Testament. Jesus' kingdom parables in Matthew 13 are a good place to start. Jesus taught that spiritual life proceeds dramatically but invisibly. It grows inexorably, like yeast working through a lump of dough. At any given moment we cannot say, "that person is in and that person is out," because God alone will do the spiritual sorting out at the end of time. Jesus portrayed God as a father with open arms. Paul dialogued with Athenian philosophers, quoted secular poets, and progressively laid out the implications of following Jesus in the lecture hall of Tyrannus in Ephesus for two years. Peter counseled his readers to have ready answers for anyone asking about their faith, and both he and Jesus declared that a life of good works is one of the loudest ways to "speak" the good news.

In Pursuit of the One

Relationships are more challenging than transactions. They take longer and are potentially far messier. It always costs something to go on a sheep hunt. Jesus'original listeners knew he wasn't advocating the abandonment of the sheep that were still in the fold. Shepherds worked in teams. Therefore, several would watch over the ninety-nine while another would pursue the one. Apart from a concerted effort to establish a relationship with a missing sheep, the ninety-nine would soon conclude that it is "normal" to be one short of one hundred. Ultimately it is the shepherd's willingness to go looking for the missing sheep that gives the other ninety-nine their security. Every human sheep now knows, "The shepherd would do that for *me* if I become the one who is lost."

It cannot be denied that 99 percent of the energy invested in most local churches concerns the ninety-nine who are already on site. Congregations are skilled at tinkering with security systems for people who are already safe. Let's be honest. Shouldn't those numbers be reversed? Would our willingness to pay the price for an ongoing ministry of human search-and-rescue escalate if we appropriately concluded that the church, numerically, is more like the one, and that those adrift in our culture are the ninety-nine? What will it take for us to see the need?

One spring evening the elders of our church gathered at seven o'clock for their monthly meeting. "Let's do something a bit different for our prayer time," I began. Like good Westerners every single one of us had arrived as a solo driver. "You have forty-five minutes. Please get into your car—no music or radio, please—and drive two miles south of the church." That would bring us all to the intersection of a U.S. highway and the interstate loop around Indianapolis. "Park your car outside a restaurant, a store, a mall or any place that you see people. Just watch them. Who do you see? Pray for them. Ask God what we need to do in order to bring the good news to the people you see tonight."

An hour later we reassembled and told our stories. It had been stunning to see how many people were *alone*. How many children were out by themselves. How many adults had faces that reflected boredom, anger, or grim determination to accomplish errands. How many people were speaking a language other than English. How many minorities were present just two miles from our church, but whom none of us could imagine as being drawn to our front door.

Our elders spoke of the power and freedom that came from praying for people instead of merely competing with them for parking spaces. We agreed that over the next thirty days we would find other opportunities to "people-watch"—at malls, during lunch breaks, or by tuning in to an hour of MTV. And we would ask God that same question: "What would it take, and what kind of church would we need to be, to reach those who are just down the street but may know nothing of your love?"

We didn't design new programs that night. First we simply tried to see. Our hearts did come closer, I believe, to the heart of God.

We began to feel the sense of urgency that motivates the Shepherd who knows his flock is incomplete.

The Task of Restoration

There is often a substantial gulf between a personal willingness to share our spiritual stories and the long-term challenge of bringing someone over and around the numerous obstacles to discipleship. Evangelism is not a single event; it is not merely an invitation extended several times. It is a lengthy relational process that incorporates listening, hearing, speaking, praying, and encouraging. This is reflected in the intermediate "gap" that follows:

From: I tend to be reluctant when it comes to sharing the good news, due to inexperience, fear and/or not knowing how to answer spiritual questions.

To: Relying upon God working in me I frequently share my faith and can effectively and lovingly dialogue with those who are exploring the claims of Christianity.

Looking for a lost sheep in Palestine has never been a walk in the park. The search may take days. The land is extremely dry.

Most shepherds who are searching in the midst of such conditions will think to themselves, "I hope I find the sheep—and I pray that it's already dead." Then the shepherd can bring back an ear or a foot and say, "Here is it. I found it. Job over. There's nothing left to do."

But that's not how Jesus' story goes. When the shepherd finds the lost sheep, it is not only alive; he "*joyfully* puts it on his shoulders and goes home." At this point he has a bulky creature known for its feisty unpredictability, its four feet bound together, resting on his neck as he walks back through the wilderness. Jesus is telling us that when the one who is lost has been found, the task of restoration has just begun. The process of bringing broken human lives into God's wholeness requires a lifetime.

211

Two Barriers to Cross

Jesus' Great Commission (Mt 28:19,20) specifies our task: "make disciples." It defines the prevailing circumstances: "as you go." It establishes the expectation of affiliation with the church: "baptizing them in the name of the Father and of the Son and of the Holy Spirit." It acknowledges the need for aspiring disciples to grow in spiritual certainty: "teaching them to obey everything I have commanded you." Those who are being called and equipped to be lifelong learners of Jesus, in other words, have to cross two barriers—a barrier of affiliation and a barrier of spiritual understanding.

Where precisely are the sheep that God longs to bring into our congregations? Our mission is clarified by a simple diagram that generates four quadrants. The vertical axis denotes affiliation or assimilation. Those on the left side of the line are unchurched. They do not "belong" to the body of Christ in the sense of meaningful

Quadrant 4 Unchurched Christians	Quadrant 1 Disciples
Affiliation	Affiliation
Spiritual Understanding	**Spiritual Understanding**
Quadrant 3 Unchurched Seekers	Quadrant 2 Unconvinced Church Members

participation. Those on the right side are "churched" in the sense that they have been incorporated into a regular gathering of Christians.

The horizontal axis denotes spiritual insight or understanding. When those below the line are asked, "Who is your Lord?" they identify a master other than Jesus, or admit their ongoing doubt, confusion, or apathy concerning this question. Those above the line have knowingly received Christ's offer of new life and are aware of his claim on every detail of their existence.

How then should we identify the quadrants? Quadrant 1 is our target space. It connotes a *disciple*—an intentional imitator of Jesus who is actively involved in transforming relationships with other disciples. Quadrant 2 is reserved for *unconvinced church members*. These individuals occupy pews but, consciously or unconsciously, have never resolved to pursue Jesus' version of the good life.

Quadrant 3 is populated by *unchurched seekers*. These men and women have no relationships of an intentionally spiritual nature with Christians. Their search for personal security and significance may include a commitment to achievement, to hedonism, to Buddha, to philanthropy, to cynicism, or to any of a number of other worldviews that may or may not promise optimism or hope.

In Quadrant 4 we find *unchurched Christians*—including some who are unaffiliated on a temporary basis and others who are pursuing solo Christianity as a way of life. As many as 20 percent of America's Christians decline active church involvement. Without begrudging their apparent spiritual security, it is the thesis of this book that growth as a disciple of Jesus demands ongoing participation in a set of redemptive personal relationships. There is no normal Christian life outside the church.

Pathways to Discipleship

What is the task of evangelism? Our mission is to bring greater and greater numbers of people into Quadrant 1. One tactic or one initiative cannot simultaneously reach every target audience. It's immediately apparent that there are four pathways by which the recruiting of new disciples might happen, three of which are preferable:

(1) *In-House Spiritual Growth* (Quadrant 2 to Quadrant 1). Our own congregations are fields that are ripe for harvest. Individuals who have joined the church but not joined the family of God must be challenged to make progress across the barrier of spiritual understanding.

(2) *Transfer or Reactivation Growth* (Quadrant 4 to Quadrant 1). Spiritually convinced people must be called and challenged to cross the barrier of affiliation into relationship with members of the body of Christ.

(3) *Conversion Growth* (Quadrant 3 to Quadrant 1). Because two different barriers must be crossed, bringing the unchurched-and-unconvinced person to a relationship with Jesus is an arduous undertaking, requiring a considerable investment of patience, love, prayer, strategic planning, and relational sensitivity. Churches need to discover the power of "side-door evangelism"—inviting unchurched people into existing small groups and ministry teams. It is in the context of thriving relationships—worshipping, serving, studying, or just walking alongside active disciples—that many unchurched people first experience the reality of the good news. What does this mean? Church must not be "for the convinced only."

(4) *Transient Growth* (Quadrant 1 to Quadrant 1). This is the least desirable means of experiencing church growth; we cannot in good conscience even call it a fulfillment of the Great Commission. By transient growth we mean the rotation of sheep from one flock to another (a.k.a., "church hopping"). Research reveals that more

than 90 percent of the rapid growth of America's mega churches is actually the result of attracting and incorporating spiritually convinced men and women who are already actively involved in other congregations. The churches that donate their members to enable this kind of numerical growth prefer a less charitable label for this phenomenon: "sheep stealing."

Is the proliferation of mega churches a sign of spiritual vitality, or evidence of dysfunction in American Christianity? The answer is probably "yes" to both options. The jury will be out for at least the first quarter of the twenty-first century. In the meantime we can be sure that mega churches are not a magical answer to the challenge of the Great Commission. When Jesus ascended into heaven he left behind a congregation of 120 people, a flock that would hardly merit a blip on today's ecclesiastical radar screen. The church at Jerusalem, however, was comprised of *120 seriously committed disciples*. Quite simply they changed the world. We are the ongoing evidence of their radical devotion.

The Applause of Heaven

Growing maturity in the fifth mark embodies a remarkable transition. Faith-sharing is no longer an activity to be pursued, but a lifestyle to be lived.

From: I share the good news from the confines of my faith.

To: Freed by the love of Christ, I share his good news with his grace.

There is no party like the kind of party that celebrates the adoption of a new member of God's family. At the end of Jesus' parable, there is much joy. "He [the shepherd who has restored the lost sheep] calls his friends and neighbors together and says, 'Rejoice with me'" (Lk 15:6). I've always thought this verse a bit strange. I can't imagine telephoning the neighbors on my street and saying, "You'll never believe it, but I finally found my weed eater. It was right behind my snow shovel the whole time! How about coming over for some burgers this evening?"

Once again Kenneth Bailey supplies a needed insight. In Palestine, ten to twenty families would jointly own a flock of sheep. So if one sheep became lost, it was everyone's loss. And if that sheep were found, it was everybody's victory. Anyone who stands outside God's family constitutes a loss for all of us (Concordia Publishing House, 1973, p. 23).

Since heaven's applause is loudest for those who are awakening to an awareness of God's love, we are in serious need of rethinking our relationships. How do I see the people around me? Are they competitors I need to beat? Are they annoyances I need to avoid? Are they customers I need to market? Or are they people who at the end of every day need essentially one thing—the wholeness of being in a genuine relationship with Jesus Christ?

How shall we reach them?

A few years back I had a chance to visit the biggest tree in the world. It's the sequoia named The General Sherman, which is found in Sequoia National Park high up on a Sierra Nevada mountainside. The numbers associated with this tree are staggering. It's as high as a 28-story building. At its base its trunk is thirty-six-and-a-half feet wide. Along with a few thousand other gigantic sequoias that are found only in one part of eastern California, it's also a national treasure and has to be protected. Therefore there's a fence around the General Sherman. I wasn't allowed to touch it.

By contrast I can look outside my window right now and see a number of sugar maples. They are leafy green every summer and display the most beautiful reds and oranges every fall. These trees will never grow like sequoias. They will never become colossally self-absorbed with their own magnificence. They are much more successful than that. Billions of sugar maples dot the entire eastern half of the United States. Why? Because maple trees don't grow by getting fatter. They grow by producing more maple trees. You know what the best part is? I can touch the maple trees outside my window any time I want.

God's call is not that our churches become fatter. God yearns for us to be lavishly fruitful—one human life at a time—reproducing the work of the Holy Spirit to the ends of the earth and to the very end of time.

Questions for Further Exploration

Personal, one-on-one, or small groups

1. Where would you place yourself in the "gaps" on this mark—as a seeker, a beginner, an intermediate, or a mature disciple?

2. What positive and negative associations do you have with the word evangelism? As far as you can discern, how did these originate?

3. What individuals helped you come to faith in Christ? How, specifically, did they "voice" the good news to you?

4. Faith-sharing involves varying degrees of motivation, skill training, confidence, and risk-taking. Assess your personal readiness in each realm. Assign yourself a number from 1 (low) to 10 for each area.

_____ **Motivation:** *I am eager to help others find real life in Christ.*

_____ **Skill Training:** *I know how to share the basics of the gospel.*

_____ **Confidence:** *I am ready and able to be used by God.*

_____ **Risk-taking:** *I am willing to step out on a limb to serve God.*

Getting Started

On Your Own

Most of us don't have to be experts on the New Testament story of Jesus, but we do need to be able to articulate our own spiritual story as an illustration of Christ's transforming power. Briefly write out your own story in three parts:

B.C.

Tell something about the nature of your life prior to becoming a follower of Christ. If you cannot recall a "B.C." period, describe a time in which you drifted away from his lordship.

Wake up

Identify at least one defining event that helped establish or cement your relationship with Christ. Tell why you decided to trust him, and how you did it.

Today

Describe one place where God is at work in your life right now. How is trusting Christ transforming you? What progress are you able to see?

As a Congregation

Using the illustration of the 4 quadrants, evaluate your congregation's evangelistic initiatives. Which kind of growth are you currently targeting? Which kind of growth has been most typical during the past five years?

13

A SPIRIT OF SERVANTHOOD AND STEWARDSHIP

We live as servants of God and each other, doing
good through the gifts the Spirit has given us, living
generously and simply, seeking to bring about the
fullest expression of God's rule in our culture.

*"In the same way, any of you who does not give up
everything he has cannot be my disciple."*

(Luke 14:33)

James Cameron's recent movie version of the sinking of the
Titanic is exceptional in that it focuses on a part of the *Titanic*
story that every previous film had ignored: the reality of the
hundreds of passengers who were still alive and screaming for
help in the freezing waters of the Atlantic long after the ship had
disappeared.

The raw numbers of the *Titanic* disaster were as chilling as the
water. There were 2,223 souls on board when the boat hit the ice-
berg. The ship was equipped with twenty lifeboats, having a total
capacity of 1,178. Even though there was room for more than half

the passengers to be saved, a mere 705 were rescued. The difference between the lifeboat capacity of 1,178 and 705 is 473. At least that many people were still alive and thrashing about in the water for up to forty minutes after the Titanic sank. Why didn't the lifeboats, which were only partially filled, go back to rescue them?

We know the answer to that question. According to *Titanic: An Illustrated History*, in sworn testimony presented in the hearings that followed the disaster, conversations in the lifeboats were reconstructed. In lifeboat number one, Charles Hendricksen proposed going back to pick up some of those who were in the water. But Lady Duff Gordon muttered something about the danger of being swamped. Her husband, Sir Cosmo Gordon, offered five pounds to each of the crewmen aboard not to row them back. The other male passengers agreed that a rescue would be dangerous. Lifeboat number 1 held only twelve people. It could have carried forty (Hyperion, 1992, p. 142ff).

In lifeboat number 8 several passengers strenuously pressed for going back. One said out loud that he would rather die with those in the water than row off and be safe, but the majority overruled him. Quartermaster Hichens graphically described what would happen if they returned. Desperate, drowning people would surely capsize them. "It's no use going back for a lot of stiffs," he said.

One of the lifeboats, which was filling with water, needed to be bailed out. A crewmember asked to borrow the hat of one of the men who was there so he could start bailing, but the man refused. Even though he was soaked to the skin with freezing water, the man said, "If I give you my hat, I might catch cold in the night air." In the end, only two lifeboats went back—numbers 4 and 14. By the time they responded they were able to save only three people.

Taking up God's Agenda

What is most disturbing about those lifeboat conversations is how similar they are to discussions that are regularly heard within the walls of churches—Christians who are debating whether they should extend care to those in the inner city, or reach out to the rural poor, or target the needs of people screaming for financial help, or serve as advocates for those who are too small or too silent to have a voice of their own. "We can't go help those people. We don't have a budget for that. They'll pull us under. They're not like us. Isn't there some agency that's supposed to help? It's probably too late, anyway. They're just a bunch of stiffs. We have to take care of *us*."

The spirit of servanthood and stewardship acknowledges a different call. Our lifelong job assignment is not to take care of us. It is to lay down our agendas to take up the agenda of our Lord. Disciples are increasingly in awe of the fact that all of life is a gift. Every possession, every relationship and every breath originates from the hand of God. Therefore the only lifestyle that is rational—that is, that corresponds to reality—is that of the servant, the one whose joy increasingly becomes the result of seeking someone else's joy.

Our security becomes bound up not in trying to "be somebody," but in recognizing that we already are God's somebodies. As we grasp that our money, our time, our sexuality, our talents, our dreams and everything else we value are not really ours but are gifts from God, we can relax our tight grip on these treasures and let them be multiplied as gifts to others.

Identifying with Jesus

Jesus' heart was consistently aligned to meet the needs of other people. His life from beginning to end was intentionally outward-focused: "For even the Son of Man did not come to be served, but to serve, and to give his life as a ransom for many" (Mk 10:45). As we noted in Chapter 3, Jesus' identity was that of a servant. Therefore the one who imitates Jesus must also choose to serve as a way of life.

221

It's not an accident that the "discipleship marks" recognized at our church are intentionally linked to the human body. They are easier to remember that way.

Heart. Mind. Arms. Knees. Voice. It's become natural to point to our own bodies as we recite the effects of Jesus' life within us. The mark that breaks the pattern is number 6. What body part should be associated with the servant lifestyle, in which generous giving and good works get equal time with the good news? It occurred to me that people in the ancient Near East had the answer.

They understood the seat of emotions (and thus the source of compassion) to be the *splanchnon*, the Greek word for bowels and intestines, which roughly corresponds to "guts." The translators of the King James Version preserved this meaning in their rendering of I John 3:17: "If anyone hath this world's goods and sees his brother in need but does not open up his bowels of compassion for him, how can the love of God be in him?" Our leaders pondered the possibilities for less than a minute before concluding, "Let's not go there." The more nebulous word "spirit" is the one we chose.

Ten Dollars Is Ten Dollars

Closing the gap regarding the first mark of a disciple (from many possible lords to the singular lordship of Jesus) is the most important step that a seeker can possibly take. Closing the seeker's gap regarding the sixth mark, however, is almost certainly the most difficult:

From: I don't recognize the promise of contentment in Christ and therefore have not given my life to him.

To: I receive Christ as my path to real contentment.

In American culture money is the idol that steals our hearts from God. Making money is the idolatrous alternative to living as servants. Personal progress is measured by our accelerating ability to buy what we do not need. Society has succumbed to the myth that money can actually deliver the things it promises—happiness, security, relationships, and confidence.

Consider the experience of Stumpy and Martha. Year after year they attended the fair in their home state, and every summer it was the same story: Stumpy was tantalized by the old-fashioned bi-plane in which anybody could take a ride for ten dollars, and Martha was disgusted by such an obvious waste of money. "Ten dollars is ten dollars," she would always say. And Stumpy would go home without his airplane ride.

One year Stumpy said, "Martha, there's that bi-plane again. I am eighty-one years old and this year I want to go for a ride." Martha bristled, "There you go again. Don't you realize that ten dollars is ten dollars?" At this point the man who owned the bi-plane, and who had heard this conversation as far back as he could remember, intervened. "Listen, you two, I'll make you a deal. I'll give you both a ride *for free* if you promise not to say anything during the flight. If you speak even one word, I'll charge you the ten dollars." Stumpy and Martha thought that sounded fair, and off they went.

The pilot put on quite a show. He took his plane through banks and spins and loop-the-loops, and then did the whole thing over again. Amazingly, he never heard a single word. When the plane landed he looked over at Stumpy and said, "I'll have to admit I'm impressed. You never spoke even once." "Well," said Stumpy, "I was going to say something when Martha fell out of the plane, but ten dollars is ten dollars."

If there's one thing that Americans understand, it's the value of money. If there's one thing that Americans fundamentally misunderstand, it's the value of God. In the marketplace theology of our times we may trust God to be there; we may trust God to hear our prayers; we may even trust God with getting us to heaven after we die. But the toughest challenge for the would-be disciple is trusting that God *provides*—that God will actually come through by supplying us with what we need, when we need it.

Who's In Charge?

Four key questions help us discern our personal commitment to the sixth mark. We must begin by asking, *Who's in Charge?* Who do I think is in charge of making life's rules? Who gets to say, "This is what success looks like, and this is what constitutes the good life"?

Paul writes in I Timothy 6:17, "Command those who are rich in this present world not to be arrogant nor to put their hope in wealth, which is so uncertain, but to put their hope in God, who richly provides us with everything for our enjoyment." God alone declares the meaning of success. We must accept no alternatives. After all, it's possible to feel great about making significant progress in a race that God has assured us is not worth winning.

We don't have to do exegetical backflips to agree that this verse is addressed to us. From a global perspective, if you could afford to buy this book, then you are among "those who are rich in this present world." If most of us cleaned out our closets this afternoon and set aside what we know we will never use again, our castoffs would be considered treasures by two-thirds of the world's population. The Bible assures us that there's nothing inherently wrong with being rich. But it also tells us that being rich is inherently dangerous. We who are used to nice things are powerfully tempted to associate our happiness with the continued accumulation of nice things. Our choices come down to putting our hope in money, which, as Paul says, "is so uncertain," or putting our hope in God, who "richly provides us with everything for our enjoyment."

So who's in charge? In this world and the next, Christ is in charge. Our standard of living must never supplant his throne. Jesus alone is the one who has the power to declare, "This is what's going to last forever."

Where's Home?

Our convictions concerning the lordship of Jesus become crucially important when we consider our second question: *Where's Home?* To put it another way, are we currently investing our service and accumulating our treasure in the right location? Disciples at the beginning of their journey of contentment have to make this important shift:

From: I serve and give to Jesus and others of my time, resources, and energy when it is convenient.

To: Because of God's commands, I serve and give to Jesus and others a portion of my time, resources and energy even when I don't feel like it.

The key to this transition is an underlying shift of priorities—from investing in the only world we have ever known to investing in a future world that God assures us has superior value.

Nebraska is a place that I have never called home. It is a Great Plains state that I have experienced from time to time on my way to somewhere else. The Nebraska locale that I happen to know best is a small town along Interstate 80 called North Platte. To date I've been to North Platte on three occasions. Once I stopped there to fill my gas tank and stretch my legs—after which I kept right on driving.

Back in college I made a second visit, one that lasted a good deal longer. I was attending a retreat at a nearby camp when the North Platte River reached flood stage and began overflowing its banks. The kids in our college group became a rescue squad, filling sandbags to keep the water from inundating the camp. My wife-to-be was also part of that group, although at that time we weren't even dating. I couldn't help noticing, however, "There stands a woman who knows how to bag sand"—something that I filed away for future consideration.

225

My third adventure in North Platte was entirely unplanned. Coming back from a high school work camp trip to Colorado, one of our vans suddenly broke down—one mile from the North Platte exit. A local mechanic diagnosed our problem and then got on the computer, only to discover that the one part required for the repair was available at just three sites west of the Mississippi River—in Texas, somewhere on the West coast, and in Wyoming. While the mechanic graciously made a round trip to Wyoming and then fixed our van, the leaders of our trip were marooned in North Platte, Nebraska, with a group of tired and restless teenagers for forty-eight hours. It was a dark chapter in youth ministry.

Our True Destination

Perhaps you have been a resident of North Platte and loved it. To me, that Nebraska town is an illustration of how we all are compelled to spend time in places that are not our true home. The Bible says that Christians are "aliens and strangers" in this world. This is not our true place of residence. You might say that this world is North Platte. We're only here for a short time. While we are here we are called to serve, just as we tried to help make things right by sandbagging a river. And while we are here we are likely to experience a variety of breakdowns. But no matter what, this must not be mistaken for home. We're always on our way to our true destination.

In the words of those who declined to become Jesus' disciples, "This is a hard saying" (Jn 6:60). All we have ever seen and known and experienced is this world. This is where our ambitions and our passions and our hopes and our dreams are being played out. This is where we go to school and take our vacations and keep our bank accounts. Many of us are fundamentally committed to being this-world residents. We want to run for mayor of North Platte.

But Scripture assures us that our home is somewhere else. In I Timothy 6:19, those who have become overly comfortable in this world are counseled to "lay up treasure for themselves as a firm foundation for the coming age, so that they may take hold of the life that is truly life." Where's our real home? It's heaven.

Nothing spotlights the issue of spiritual character as effectively as facing our own mortality. Those who sell life insurance know that it's absolutely necessary to talk about the reality of death. But none of us likes to speak or hear those words. An insurance agent might point to a table of financial projections and say something like, "Now, if something should happen to you, God forbid." But the truth is that God is *not* going to forbid my death. And he is not going to forbid yours. At that time we will be accountable to the One who will ask us, "What did you do with the good things that I graciously poured into your life?"

The Currency of the Next World

Sociologists are having a field day observing a new group on the American scene. They are the Children of Rich Fathers. For the first time in our history—for the first time in the history of any country—a large number of women and men, at a comparatively young age, are inheriting great wealth. By and large there is no public consensus and almost no family training in how to utilize these assets. Just after World War II 8 percent of American households were judged to have significant discretionary income. Today that number has risen to 51 percent. After basic personal and family needs have been met, what does God want us to do with the good things that have come our way?

God has granted us extraordinary freedom to bless our world. *We have the chance to be lifeboat number 4.* Myriad verses in Scripture declare that helping the poor, working for justice, and walking as servants among the powerful are priorities close to the heart of

God. Many of us are called to be volunteer home missionaries and philanthropists right now and aren't even aware of it. We are blessed to be a blessing.

I enjoy collecting paper currency from other countries. From time to time I might have some Romanian lei, a few Japanese yen, and a couple of Euros in my wallet. They're multi-colored, fun to look at, and completely worthless in the American marketplace. You can visit another country and stuff your wallet with its legal tender—but as soon as your jet lands in New York City these pieces of paper can't buy a pack of gum.

God assures us that our destination is another country. Only a fool would spend his life trying to hold on to the currency of this world, which in the next world will be powerless to buy anything. The currency of heaven is *character like that of Jesus*. Are we pursuing a path that is making us more and more like God's Son?

What's My Job?

Significant urgency is associated with question number 3: *What's My Job?* An ever-growing experience of God's faithfulness prompts the disciple's next shift:

From: I serve and give to Jesus and others a portion of my time, resources, and energy in response to God's commands.

To: Because of God's provision, I generously serve and give to Jesus and others my time, resources and energy in order to transform God's world.

How do we accumulate the lasting treasure that Paul talks about in I Timothy Chapter 6? In verse 18 he gets practical: "Command them to do good, to be rich in good deeds, and to be generous and willing to share." Lasting spiritual treasure means investing in gifts and service and acts of love that will benefit the only part of our daily reality that we know is going to last forever—*the people around us*.

228

Many of us are willing to give a portion of our lives to this job, but not our whole lives. ABC churches have tended to establish benchmarks that leave us far short of God's desires. If we contribute a tithe of our income to God's work, if we worship regularly, if we join a small group or ministry, if we occasionally provide an offering for the poor, then the rest of our money and our time belong to us. *This overtly artificial standard has no basis whatsoever in the teaching of Jesus.* Discipleship is the electrifying discovery that stewardship doesn't speak to 10 percent of life. It speaks to 100 percent of what I possess. We may be certain that when it comes to the things of God, possession should not be misunderstood as ownership. A steward is someone who is responsible for managing the property of somebody else. Why are we so staggered by the implications of the truth that 100 percent of what we have is on loan to us from God?

The Cost of Following Jesus

At the turn of the last century Ernest Shackleton, the Antarctic adventurer, placed an ad in a British newspaper that sought partners for his next expedition: "Men wanted for hazardous journey. Small wages; bitter cold; long months in complete darkness; constant danger; safe return doubtful." Shackleton didn't get many recruits. It's no wonder: He told the truth.

What would happen if our churches told the truth, loudly and boldly, about what it costs to follow Jesus? In *Turning Points*, Vaughan Roberts puts it this way: "We have managed to do something that the early Christians would not have thought possible. We have made Christianity safe, middle-class, comfortable. Even when we acknowledge [the words of Jesus], we tame them. So, self-denial becomes giving up sugar in Lent and taking up our cross means enduring back pain or having Aunt Agatha to stay at Christmas. But the words of Jesus go far deeper than that. The only ones in Palestine who were seen carrying crosses were those on their way to be executed. Jesus is saying, 'You must be willing to die for me.'" (OM Publishing, 1999, p. 190).

Servanthood and stewardship from this perspective require a value shift of monumental proportions. I can no longer agree with my culture that my life is my own, that my time is a personal possession, and that others exist for my benefit. I cannot affirm the multitude of ads that declare, "I'm worth it," "I deserve it," and "This I do for me."

Let us understand: *This is not an agenda for religious fanatics.* This is what *normal* human life was always designed to be. How is it that a tiny Albanian nun could stand before a crowded room in Washington D.C. and quietly denounce the moral ambiguity of America's President to his face? The answer is that Mother Teresa spoke with the authority of a woman whose life was in alignment with God's values. The "power people" at that gathering remained silent. They were in the overwhelmingly powerful presence of a fully surrendered life.

Was Mother Teresa a splendid aberration, or someone just like us? God crafted our minds, bodies, and emotions to be at their best when we are serving others sacrificially, just as she endeavored to transform the slums of Calcutta. It's not unlikely that some of those we know who are depressed and embittered by life arrived at their condition not because of unusual circumstances, but because they persistently passed up opportunities to help others when it was in their power to help. They hunkered down in the safety of what was predictable and comfortable, instead of investing their gifts beyond themselves.

Risking God's Resources

In his book, *Living Like Jesus*, Ron Sider points out that followers of Christ are uniquely positioned to impact the globe. Although

Christians represent less than one-third of the world's population, we annually receive two-thirds of the world's income. Incredibly, we spend 97 percent of it on ourselves. Most of the remainder goes into the hands of "rich Christians running expensive programs in their own congregations and nations" (Baker Books, 1966, p. 145).

The world has falsely pictured the Church as beggars on the verge of going out of business. Too many people have come to the conclusion that congregations are chiefly concerned with sustaining their own viability at any cost. What if Christians everywhere took the minimal step of placing 10 percent of their income at God's disposal, and what if congregations faithfully invested that sum not in the maintenance of their status quo but in reaching out to those who are drowning in poverty, addiction, and despair right now within earshot of our spiritual lifeboats? Even the most conservative estimates indicate that that response alone would wipe out the poverty of the poorest 20 percent of the earth's population.

Are we serious about changing the world?

What's my job? It's to generously share what God has shared with me. It is to risk the totality of God's resources to accomplish his purposes. God has blessed us to be a blessing. When John D. Rockefeller died his accountant was asked, "So how much did he leave?" The accountant's response was classic: "He left it all." By God's grace, however, the investment of all we are in the lives of other people for the sake of Christ is a treasure that will neither be taken away nor left behind.

What Is Success?

Who's in charge? Christ alone is in charge. *Where's home?* My true home is heaven. *What's my job?* My job is to serve as Jesus served, and to share what he has shared with me. Here's our final question: *What is success?* An ever-maturing walk with Christ helps us close this final gap:

From: Because of God's abundant provision, I generously serve and give to Jesus and others my time, resources, and energy.

To: In humility, I joyfully offer to Jesus and others the fullness of my time, resources, and energy.

What is success? On any given day there are millions of people who would define success as picking the correct numbers in this week's lottery. Such an event they would reckon as great gain. Consider Paul's counter-cultural words in I Timothy 6:6: "But godliness with contentment is great gain." The Bible declares that, if our personal ledger sheet shows the winning lottery ticket in our asset column but authentic contentment in the loss column, then our net balance would be less than zero.

How much net worth is required to experience godliness with contentment? Paul says in Chapter 6, verse 8, "But if we have food and clothing, we will be content with that." Contentment is the sum of an equation: Basic needs plus eternal perspective plus wholehearted abandonment to Jesus Christ and his ways. That is the final measure of human success.

Jesus consistently throws down the gauntlet. He forces us to choose between what we think is treasure and what he thinks is treasure. What hangs in the balance is whether we will experience the reality of trusting God. Our call is to stare down at least four "trust busters." They form an imposing lineup: *phobia, amnesia, inertia,* and *mañana.* These are the four chief obstacles to living out a spirit of servanthood and stewardship.

The God Who Provides

Phobia, or fear, always tops the list. It's fair to say that a number of people who were riding the crest of the American economic wave just a few years ago are now in a serious wrestling match with fear. We have been living in amazing times. The last twenty years of the

232

twentieth century have witnessed the greatest legal creation of personal wealth in human history. Americans have amassed somewhere between seven and ten trillion dollars, and much of that is currently being passed precariously from one generation to another. Nevertheless, global uncertainties and the grim specter of personal debt have generated a climate of deep anxiety.

What is the antidote? Our call is straightforward: *As a daily lifestyle* we must trust that God is a God who provides. Jesus declared in the Sermon on the Mount, "Therefore I tell you, do not worry about your life, what you will eat or drink, or about your body, what you will wear. Isn't life more important than food, and the body more important than clothes? Look at the birds of the air; they do not sow or reap or stow away in barns, and yet your heavenly Father feeds them. Are you not much more valuable than they? Which of you by worrying can add a single hour to his life?" He continued, "So do not worry, saying, 'What shall we eat?' or 'What shall we drink?' or 'What shall we wear?' For the pagans run after all these things, and your heavenly Father knows that you need them. But seek first his kingdom and his righteousness, and all these things will be given to you as well" (Mt 6:25–33).

Economic struggles are among our greatest spiritual learning opportunities. One of the reasons we have to keep learning the same lessons of trust is that we suffer spiritual *amnesia*. We keep forgetting God's assurances. Observers estimate that every day we are bombarded with 16,000 advertisements, each of which is geared to pull us toward a new purchase or experience or investment.

Who is endeavoring, on the other hand, to remind us of God's call to utilize our wealth to advance the kingdom? The silence in most congregations is deafening. In the ABC environment stewardship is merely fundraising. In the disciple-making church, stewardship is a spiritual issue—a heartfelt abandonment of the whole self to God. Our call is to remain lifelong students of what God says about managing God's resources. Otherwise we will forget everything we hear on Sunday morning as soon as we see another full-page ad for a Sunday afternoon sale.

Today not Tomorrow

The third trust buster is *inertia*, which literally means, "not working" or "not going forward." Most of us reach a place of personal comfort with regard to our level of servanthood and sacrifice, and then resist change. Inertia is the assumption or the hope that I won't have to do anything costly to demonstrate my trust in God. Perhaps everything will work out all by itself.

During my first dozen years of ministry I never preached a single sermon nor taught a single Bible study encouraging those in my congregation to be lavishly generous with their resources. Why the silence? For the first twelve years of my ministry I myself was fearfully maintaining control of every dime. A woman once approached Gandhi and said, "Mahatma, tell my son that he shouldn't be eating sugar." Gandhi told her to come back in seven days. At that point he sat with her little boy and gently made a case not to eat sugar. The woman asked, "Why didn't you just tell him that seven days ago?" "Seven days ago," said Gandhi, "I was still eating sugar myself." For twelve years I knew I had no grounds on which to say that God provides for those who trust him; I myself had refused to exercise such trust.

Frankly I tripped over the math. I couldn't picture how God would come through. I recoiled from the hard choices and the sacrifices necessary to realign our family budget. In my head I cherished the conviction that Matthew 6:33 speaks the truth—that seeking God's kingdom above everything else is the ultimate human security. But for all intents and purposes, I didn't actually believe in the God whose existence I declared. When push came to shove, *I didn't reckon him worthy of trust.*

God used a Barnabas to change my life. Another pastor became my Son of Encouragement in the realm of money. More than anything else, he was a living model that God kept his promises. Choosing to be generous was both terrifying and exhilarating. Only on the other side of that decision did our family come to realize the degree to which God takes care of those who rely on him. Sacrifice is giving up something we love for the sake of something we love even more.

What's the last lethal opponent to trust? *Mañana.* Tomorrow. "These are valid insights. In fact, our church needs to shift the way we imitate the generosity of Jesus. Let's do that...just after the holidays. Sometime in the future, when we've done sufficient studying, we need to sit down and figure out how to respond." But tomorrow is too late. We can hear the cries of those still in the water. What is the antidote to *mañana*? We must trust God *today*.

By God's grace—endowed with his gifts and assured of strength—let's row toward those in need.

Questions for Further Exploration

Personal, one-on-one, or small groups
1. Where would you place yourself in the "gaps" on this mark—as a seeker, a beginner, an intermediate, or a mature disciple?

2. What is your deepest fear, or phobia, about risking your resources for God?

3. How does the notion of heaven as your true home affect your daily life? When was the last time you made a this-world decision based on next-world considerations?

4. Where do you think your church tends to let people off the hook when it comes to embodying servanthood and stewardship?

5. What one activity or commitment—if practiced by the great majority of Christian disciples—would most move or impress non-Christians to consider the claims of Christ?

Getting Started

On Your Own

Do a personal inventory of your current priorities based on three simple questions: What do I think about? On what do I spend my money? Where do I invest my time? Then ask yourself: *Are these the thoughts, investments, and commitments that I would want to be embracing during the final week of my life?* What's preventing you from being sold out to God's priorities?

As a Congregation

Evaluate your church's stewardship sermons and communications of the past three years. Do they reflect an emphasis on fundraising or a call to a whole-life spiritual commitment? What shifts would need to be made—not merely in language but in goals, motivations, and illustrations—to align with the teaching of Jesus in the Sermon on the Mount (*see especially* Mt 6)?

14

THE HABITS OF A DISCIPLE-MAKING CHURCH

Nothing clears the mind as effectively as a disaster. Often we discover the roots of our disaster-producing behaviors only by looking in the rear view mirror. The detailed inquiry that followed the sinking of the *Titanic* included the public grilling of Captain Henry Clarke. He had authorized the sailing of the ship—even though when it left on its maiden voyage there had been exactly one lifeboat drill, involving just two boats and a handpicked crew.

The prosecutor bore down on Captain Clarke. "Did you think your system was satisfactory before the *Titanic* disaster?" He answered, "No, sir." "Then why did you do it?" Clarke answered, "Because it was the custom." "Do you follow a custom because it is bad?" Clarke replied, "Well, I am a civil servant, sir, and custom guides us a good bit."

Let's be honest. Custom guides all of us a good bit. So what if our customs are found to be counter-productive to our most cherished goals?

We should determine to change our customs.

If this is the point at which you'd welcome an itemized, 12-month action plan to inject discipleship into the aorta of your church, disappointment awaits you. The New Testament has provided no such plan. Nor should we create one and market it as a set of principles to guide succeeding generations. Jesus gave us a comprehensive but nonspecific vision at the end of his ministry on earth: "Go multiply disciples in every place on earth." Those are the only instructions we need.

At least 80 percent of American congregations have failed to enroll in the fulfillment of their Lord's primary vision. Custom guides them a good bit—customs of inner-directedness, self-preservation, and continual fixation on the ABCs of attendance, building, and cash. How can the power of the Holy Spirit be released to transform ecclesiastical dry bones into life-giving vitality?

We need to adopt the customs or habits of the disciple-making church.

These turn out to be far more than a list of strategies for the next season of congregational life. The following seven points represent the fundamental shifts that are required to help a group of growing disciples imitate the *whole life* of Jesus, in all of its balance and beauty.

1. Stay Centered through Prayer and Discernment

How fast can we go in our efforts to transform the culture of our church? No faster than we can go on our knees.

Prayer must not be a perfunctory seeking of God's blessing on our work. Our work itself is prayer—sustained waiting, listening, and calling on the name of the Lord.

The crucial event in our congregation's transition to a disciple-making focus was what we called our Year of Discernment. We chose to set aside an entire year (it actually became fourteen months) to listen for God's direction. We hired an outside consultant to help us—not to give us answers, but to keep us on track. The temptation was to rush forward to generate a list of tactics. This, of course, had been our standard operating procedure for years— church leadership retreats in which we brainstormed a list of ideas, then assigned them to a few already overwhelmed lay people and staff members. Over time we had not experienced transformation in the areas of our greatest concern. We had, however, experienced the magical reappearance of approximately the same brainstorming list every year.

The Year of Discernment featured a different approach and produced a different outcome. The entire congregation was invited to participate. We cast a vision for prayerfully waiting on God and listening carefully to each other, and then tried to practice that as a body. Thousands of hours were invested in surveys, interviews, small group interactions, large group forums...and quietness. At the end of the process we publicly affirmed a comprehensive commitment to be about one task—the multiplication of lifelong learners of Jesus—through the broad strategies of leadership development and reproducible relationships. This conclusion didn't feel imposed. It didn't have the ring of "the latest word from Mt. Sinai." The Spirit had spoken through every channel of our church. We concluded the Year of Discernment not with balloons, slogans, and a new shot of adrenaline, but with a quiet prayer service in which we gave thanks to God.

2. Embrace Discipleship as a Singular Focus

What is the work of the church? It's all about multiplying intentional imitators of Jesus Christ. That is the work that Jesus himself assigned to us. There is no Plan B.

The ABCs of our corporate existence are not trivial. We do indeed need to attend to the business of growth, finances, and facilities. *Business, however, is not our primary business*. It may be exhilarating to help people make a variety of decisions, but our unchanging call is to make disciples. That focus alone is capable of advancing God's kingdom.

It's hard not to chuckle when you see the bumper sticker that says, "Jesus is coming soon. Look busy." I wince, however, as I reflect on the number of years that my own life and spiritual leadership barely raised the bar above frantic busyness. Jesus has made it clear that some activities are fundamentally more productive than others. But only one activity is essential. It alone is worth living for and dying for. If we belong to Christ, then our life's work is to be his disciples, and to help others relentlessly pursue the same path.

3. Shift from a Strategy of Programs to a Strategy of Relationships

What should disciple-making look like at your church? This we know for sure: It should not look like a carbon copy of another "successful" congregation.

The Spirit has assembled a unique collection of leaders, spiritual gifts, resources, and opportunities to comprise the part of the body of Christ to which you have been called. Therefore the Spirit's ongoing work in your church will have a unique signature. There's a reason the New Testament is silent about the details of corporate body life. Such details are in constant transition from generation to generation, and from hemisphere to hemisphere. It shouldn't surprise us that a programmatic "kit" or list of how-to's—imported from a context blessed by leaders and resources that we will never share—tends to raise our energy level for a few months to a year, after which we find ourselves hungry for the next outside stimulus.

What should we do? Refuse to bet on programs. Invest in long-term, reproducible relationships.

What's a healthier option—asking each other if we are following the directives of the latest program, or holding each other accountable to entering and sustaining the relationships that Christ has always used to transform human beings into his image?

Who is your mentor—from whom are you learning how to live this disciple-life? Who is your apprentice—who is gaining such learning from you? Where is your small group—the company of fellow learners who are helping you stay on course? Where is your place of service—the realm where others are being blessed by the exercise of your spiritual gifts? Are all these relationships being nourished and informed by an ultimate and ongoing relationship with Jesus himself, in which you know who is in charge of your life, and therefore know whom you are called to be?

As church leaders we tend to rally people around momentary goals—this year's version of our strategic plan. That is shortsighted. Our call is to rally people around the single goal of becoming like Jesus. That alone gives meaning, clarity, and justification to our more immediate goals. The superior strategy is to rally people around the relationships that are best able to bring about our ultimate goal of Christlikeness.

How might this happen? We must relentlessly preach the vision. Continually reference the validity of reproducible relationships in sermons, in teaching, in newsletters, in conversation. Point to a real Barnabas and a real Timothy in your own life. What is seen matters more than what is said. As the core leaders of a church choose to live out transforming relationships in their own lives, disciple-making moves from theory to reality.

4. Emphasize the Marks of a Disciple instead of Behaviors

The six marks of a disciple are not activities to pursue, nor hoops to jump through so we can "get somewhere." They represent the character of Christ. When we challenge each other to pursue the six marks, we aren't prescribing a certain set of behaviors. Thinking, acting, and being like Jesus entails a much more rigorous commitment than a few repeated activities, no matter how much honor we associate with such behaviors.

The world is disillusioned with Christians. Jesus told his followers that their lives should be characterized by love for enemies, but we have defined success as regular attendance at Bible studies. Jesus said that we should proactively extend compassion to our neediest neighbors, but we have poured our greatest energy into the battle of hymns versus praise choruses. Jesus proclaimed that our unity would signal his existence to a watching world, but we have elevated the recitation of right theology to the highest priority.

Why are the six marks so crucial? They keep calling us beyond the merely external—our fondness for the right techniques, the right study methods, and the right answers. At the core of each one there is an element of mystery—something that defies measurement and refuses to be reduced to a set of instructions. These "marks," as such, do not appear anywhere on the pages of the New Testament. For that reason we can spend years wrangling over exactly how to categorize them. But that is not the point. Whatever words we choose to describe it, *authentic discipleship comes down to imitation of the whole character of Christ, not mastery of a few culturally approved Christian behaviors.*

It has been our aim to make the Six Marks of a Disciple our recognized church-wide curriculum. This means that every activity, ideally, should aim to deepen the personal growth of its participants in one or more of the marks.

Discipleship thus becomes the benchmark for small group leadership. When a leader asks, "What should my group be studying or accomplishing this year?" we say, "Your role is to help every person under your care grow in all six of the marks during the next twelve months." Likewise every worship service can be a fresh opportunity to teach the vision of being disciples who make disciples, and to hold up one of the marks for special emphasis.

Balance is essential. Apart from intentionally targeting six different signposts of the character of Christ, we inevitably gravitate to those aspects of discipleship to which our lives are already most aligned. I would greatly prefer to preach only two of the marks on a regular basis (both of which I can richly illustrate from my own life), while ignoring the two that quite frankly have always intimidated me. One of the leaders of our church once took me aside and said, "Thank you for challenging me to think about my Christian life more holistically. All these years I've been certain that I've been on the right track, since I'm strong in three of the marks. Now I finally see the fuller picture of what it really means, and what it will actually take, for me to be like Jesus."

5. Cultivate a Culture of Personal Discipline

One of the vivid memories that I associate with being nine years old is hearing my mom say to me, seemingly out of the blue, "Good news! I've signed you up for piano lessons beginning next week." I did not in fact receive that as particularly good news. In fact I fought my mother with everything I had in my nine-year-old arsenal—with reason, with emotion, and finally with pathetic begging. "Please don't make me do this!" I cried. But my mom was determined, and within a week I found myself sitting on a piano bench next to Mrs. Chenoweth.

To make things worse, beginning piano students don't get to play concertos by Tschaikovsky or even "The Last Train to Clarksville" by The Monkees. Piano students begin by learning the scales. This was a painful experience for me, and was certainly just as painful for my parents. But my mom was determined, so the lessons continued. Her hopes that one day I would actually love to play the piano and even become proficient at it imposed a new order on my life. My days and my weeks were shaped by the need to practice.

By the time I entered high school, it was obvious that the lessons were paying off. I had mastered a repertoire of classical music. I auditioned for regional judges and earned surprisingly good reviews. I even played the piano for fun. But high school is a busy time of life. I asked for a breather. "How about if I quit taking lessons just for one year, get my life together, and then I'll resume?" That's exactly what I did—and I've not taken a single lesson since. I still know how to place my hands on the keys. I still can generate a smattering of chords. But over the past thirty years my fingers have progressively forgotten how to play all those songs.

I used to have a skill. But then I stopped practicing. And now I have to ask myself: How do I know that the same thing isn't going to happen to my relationship with God?

God's promise that he will be faithful to me is my only real guarantee that I will still be walking with him one year from today. But something else is true. My determination to be disciplined in my spiritual life—in other words, not to stop practicing—is the only way for me to experience the fullness of God's faithfulness.

Discipline is necessary to please God. What is the purpose of life? It's to be a lifelong learner of Jesus Christ who helps reproduce other lifelong learners. What is required of a disciple? *Discipline*. That means learning how to order my life so that I stay on God's path even when I start thinking that what I really need right now is a breather. A disciplined walk with God offers us hope that next week can be better than this last week, and the week after that better still.

Discipline, however, is difficult. In some contexts the word has even come to be synonymous with "punishment." For some of us, a whole week of spiritual discipline sounds about as much as fun as going to the motor vehicle department seven days in a row. Why is this true? All of us have allowed large portions of our lives to become comfortably adjusted to our own agendas. As soon as we start grasping God's agenda for our lives, we begin to realize the depth of change and the degree of realignment that lies before us. Discipline is the day-by-day process of getting from this moment to a future moment when I'm going to look a lot more like Jesus. That trip is definitely going to be challenging.

We're going to have to learn to play the scales. What does that mean with regard to Christian spirituality? Discipline is not sheer guesswork. First we acknowledge the basics of growing a heart for Christ alone, a mind transformed by the Word, arms of love, knees for prayer, a voice to speak the good news, and a spirit of servant-hood and stewardship. Then we challenge ourselves regularly with these questions: *Am I a living model of these six marks?* To what degree am I fully committed to following Jesus in these areas of my life? What actions do I need to take in order to close the gaps?

This is not the same thing as asking, "Can I recite these six marks?" Nor are we asking, "Are these the rules for my life when I'm consciously trying to be religious?" When I go to work on Monday, do I follow a different set of rules? When I'm on the phone in one of those uncomfortable conversations with an extended family member, do I suddenly switch to another set of values? What priorities take over when I'm sitting on the couch holding the remote control? Spiritual discipline means we practice just one set of scales for every area of life.

Discipline also requires a plan. It's not sufficient to say, "Well, this is just who I am right now." Discipline demands that we look at God's expectations for our lives and then devise tactics to align ourselves with them. How might that happen as a congregational strategy?

6. Utilize the Power of a PDP—A Personal Development Plan

The favorite game of American Christianity is *Let's Make a Deal with God*. Remember how Monty Hall's game show worked? You already had something in your hand—an envelope maybe, with a couple of bucks. You could hold on to that, or you could trade it for what Jay had in the box—or risk everything and take whatever was hiding behind door number two. The problem is that you might end up with a goat or a year's supply of a borderline breakfast cereal. Would you dare give up what you knew you already had for the possibility of something considerably better?

People who are contemplating a serious commitment to discipleship frequently ask, "So what's behind door number two? If I trust God, will he give me exactly what I'm asking for?" That's a great question. Here's the answer: *God doesn't make deals*. What God declares is that we need to give up what we're holding on to—all of our little bargaining chips and the things that we have assumed are going to give us spiritual leverage. Trusting God means giving up control of our own situations. God doesn't promise that he will give us exactly what we have been dreaming about. He does promise that he will give us something much better than what we're currently holding.

What disciples have learned over many centuries is that this process of giving up is precisely that—a process. Spiritual beginners do not graduate to maturity in a matter of weeks or even years. Hence it is crucial for church leaders to do two things: to hold out the vision for imitating the whole life of Jesus, while simultaneously showing how this might be accomplished in stages or steps—progressively closing the gaps in each of the six marks.

A PDP or personal development plan is an effective tool for making progress. Each year in our church we devote a Sunday morning to presenting and modeling how any individual, regardless of their current spot on the discipleship path, can establish a personal strategy for spiritual growth in the year ahead.

Some people hear this challenge and inwardly groan. They take one look at the six marks of a disciple and conclude, "There's no way. The bar is set too high. I already feel like a spiritual preschooler. Why should I put goals down on a piece of paper that will only reinforce the fact that I'm a failure?"

Other listeners tend to be delirious. "Yes! Bring it on. There's nothing more satisfying than generating another list of spiritual activities." The problem, of course, is that spiritual growth can never be captured by a list of things to do, and none of us will ever get closer to God by piling on more activities, even if we happen to do them in the name of Jesus.

Here's the good news: We can indeed go forward with Christ, even if we're so discouraged that we can't see how that could possibly happen. And we can indeed receive God's gifts of fullness and freedom, even without over-functioning or over-programming our spiritual lives. We cannot deserve and we cannot earn what God wants to give to us for free.

The purpose of a PDP is not to prove that we are either spiritual champions or hopeless slackers. Nor is it to inspire in us a whole new season of frenetic doing without our ever becoming what God wants us to be. A PDP is essentially a means of receiving God's grace. It places us within reach of the outstretched arms of the One who loves us. It helps us identify the places where we most need God's fullness and transformation right now—the kinds of changes that God alone can bring about—and then shows us what activities we need to undertake in order to better receive his gifts of healing.

Generally this is the juncture where churches make a colossal mistake. *We let people off the book*.

Church leaders will say something like, "All you need to know is that God loves you. He really loves you. Somehow everything is going to work out." But we can't afford to be so vague. There's too much at stake. If you're not working on a plan and a whole pattern of life for following Jesus, then you will only follow him where the path makes sense to you, and where the footing is comfortable—and consequently miss out on life's greatest adventure, and the very reason you were born.

A plan for spiritual growth can take many forms. Note on this sample PDP that we encouraged people to identify at least one area of life where there was a clear conviction of being less than what God had called them to be, or where they sensed God's call to break loose, or to experience greater fullness. We included a partial list of such areas for personal growth and even a few proposed action steps.

Regardless of our needs, we don't need to bargain with God. God is ready and willing to deal with us regarding our most difficult and intimate concerns. A PDP is a way of identifying such areas of action and saying, "By God's grace, I'm going to do something about this." What are the steps we would then need to take?

We commit to five actions. First we **pray**. "God, where do you want to be at work in my life right now?" It may take a number of days, but gradually we will arrive at the second step. We **discern**. If we were perfectly honest we would have to survey the six marks at any given moment and say, "I need to make immediate progress in every one of them." Most of us, however, are aware of one or two areas of blockage or bondage that are like cue balls. If we get rolling in these areas, the whole "rack" will be broken. Receiving God's forgiveness or accepting God's grace are frequently experienced in just such a manner. They break the rack. Such actions have the capacity to transform everything else we are facing.

Next we **choose**. This doesn't mean generating a new laundry list of things to do. We don't suddenly switch from God's power to our own power. Carefully chosen spiritual activities, however, put us at God's disposal. They place us in God's presence so God can be at work. Entering a discipling relationship, for example, is not itself an act of healing—but it can ultimately bring about remarkable progress in our walk with Christ.

Next we need to **commit**. With God's guidance, what are my specific intentions and my timetable for moving forward? If we write the words, "I've firmly decided that someday I'm going to do something about this area in my life," then we've not created an appropriate PDP. We need to craft a brief but specific action plan—one that will see us through to the end. Leadership guru Max Dupree has said that he never wants to be known as a world champion in the 95-yard dash. If we aren't able or willing to make it through that final five yards, then the preceding 95 yards will have little meaning.

Fifth and finally, we must be **accountable**. This is where our participation in the core relationships of discipleship makes all the difference. Who will encourage me and keep me on track if I'm spiritually walking alone? The answer is self-evident: no one. The church that is serious about spiritual growth will do everything possible to ensure that its members are in transforming relationships.

7. The Board Shifts from the ABCs to the RPMs

Issues related to attendance, building, and cash must properly come before the average church board on a regular basis. But they must not be allowed to dominate the agenda.

The board of a disciple-making church is primarily focused on providing for the fullest congregational expression of a different acronym. RPM stands for reproducible relationships, permission to do ministry, and a master plan for discipleship. The board must be the preserver of the congregation's trust that no alternative to the mission of discipleship will ever be pursued; that Spirit-empowered individuals will always be granted the freedom to carry out authentic ministry; and that the values of the six marks will always be at the root of corporate decisions.

We have discovered that the life of our board is immeasurably enriched if we commit to a pattern of mutual study and decision-making that unfolds quarter by quarter during each ministry year. While each monthly meeting has a few common features, including extended prayer and immediate ministry concerns, our times together "change shape" every three months:

Winter Quarter

Study of a particular theological issue or matter for discernment. Generally we read a book together during this time. The goal is enrichment.

Spring Quarter

Strategic planning for the year ahead, which amounts to a kind of corporate PDP. The goal is leadership.

Summer Quarter

Special study and exploration of two or three "hot button" issues that are of particular concern or interest to the church. We may produce public statements on these matters. The goal is clarification of our common life.

Fall Quarter

Discussion and decision-making in the areas of personnel, finances, and property. We establish the budget for the following year. The goal is management.

At the end of every meeting we take off the hats of our board responsibilities and return to our primary call of being disciples and ministers in the body of Christ.

A Final Word

These are the essential elements of the disciple-making church:
- A singular focus on reproducing lifelong learners of Jesus
- Reproducible relationships in the life of every disciple

- Continual fidelity to the marks of a disciple, or some credible description of the full character of Christ
- A culture of personal discipline and accountability, as expressed in strategies like a church-wide personal development plan
- A board that is committed to keeping the whole church on track

As God prompts you to move forward in your own experience of being Christ's body, be encouraged. You have all the resources you could possibly need. Remember the words of Jesus: "All authority in heaven and on earth has been given to me...And surely I am with you always, to the very end of the age" (Mt 28:18,20).

PDP
A Personal *Spiritual* Development Plan for the Coming Year

"Let us throw off everything that hinders and the sin that so easily entangles, and let us run with perseverance the race marked out for us" Hebrews 12:1.

Following Jesus is an *intentional* activity. A PDP can be a great help. Personal plans for spiritual growth may take many forms. This year you are invited to prayerfully identify at least one area of your life where you recognize your need of God's healing, God's restoration, or God's gift of freedom. Then make a commitment to pursue at least one activity that will help you experience God's transforming work in that area. Make use of the accompanying Finding Freedom and Fullness in Christ.

Pray

God, where do you want to be at work in my life right now? Where do you want to make a difference—both within me and through me?

Discern

What areas of my life need God's healing touch? Where do I sense that God's power and God's leadership in my life are being blocked?

Where do I most need spiritual freedom, and the power to trust God?

Choose

What steps can I take right now to begin trusting God in these areas? What specific activities will help?

Commit

What is my plan and my timetable for moving forward? Whose support and prayers will I count on?

Finding Freedom and Fullness in Christ

Below is a partial list of areas for spiritual growth, as well as personal action steps. Target just one or two for your PDP this year.

A Heart for Christ Alone

Greater intimacy with God   Assurance of God's presence

Fresh encounter of God   Assurance that I am God's

Trust that Jesus is the Truth

Attend a spiritual retreat weekend; request an opportunity for someone to clearly explain what it means to trust God; read a book on apologetics; sustain a daily quiet time.

A Mind Transformed by the Word

Able to know basic truths   Deeper Bible knowledge

Freedom from lust   Freedom from doubt

Assurance God loves me

Learn by teaching a Sunday School class; itemize questions and work them through with a mentor; attend an adult Bible study; memorize Bible texts; find a spiritual Barnabas.

Arms of Love

Assurance of being accepted   Wholeness in my family

Freedom from anger   Able to be a true friend

Empowerment to forgive

Meet with the healing prayer team for intercession; join a small group; seek counseling; attend a marriage enrichment weekend; read a book on personal and relational healing.

Knees for Prayer

Able to talk with God   Freedom from anxiety

Freedom from fear   Trusting God in everything

Able to give up control

Read one of a number of recommended books on the devotional life; pray daily; attend a prayer retreat; find a spiritual accountability partner; join a prayer group.

A Voice to Speak the Good News

Stand up publicly for Christ   Always speak truthfully

Help fulfill great commission   Witness to my own family

Represent God to coworkers

Participate in a mission trip; learn the basics of sharing your faith; recruit a "Timothy"; bring a neighbor to church; adopt a country for prayer and missionary support.

A Spirit of Servanthood and Stewardship

Obey God with my resources   Reach out to the poor

Risk myself for others   Trust God financially

Grow a servant's heart

Participate in a personal finances small group; join a ministry team; give God a tithe of my income; become a food bank or street mission volunteer; support a needy family.

BIBLIOGRAPHY

Bailey, Kenneth E. *The Cross and the Prodigal*. St. Louis: Concordia Publishing House, 1973.

Barclay, William, ed. *The Letters to the Corinthians*. (The Daily Study Bible Series–Rev. Ed.), Knoxville, TN: Westminster John Knox Press, 1975.

Barna, George. *Growing True Disciples*. Ventura, CA: Issachar Resources, 2000.

—. *Rechurching the Unchurched*. Ventura, CA: Issachar Resources, 2000.

Barnes, M. Craig. *Hustling God*. Grand Rapids, MI: Zondervan, 1999.

Borthwick, Paul. *Six Dangerous Questions*. Downers Grove, IL, InterVarsity Press, 1996.

Bosch, David J. *Believing in the Future*. Valley Forge, PA: Trinity Press International, 1995.

Cordeiro, Wayne. *Doing Church As a Team*. Ventura, CA: Regal Books, 2000.

Dawkins, Richard. *The Selfish Gene*. UK: Oxford University Press, 1976.

Dodd, Brian J. *The Problem With Paul*. Downers Grove, IL: InterVarsity Press, 1996.

Foster, Richard. *Prayer*. HarperSanFrancisco, 1992.

George, Carl F. *Prepare Your Church For the Future*. Grand Rapids: Fleming H. Revell, 1991.

Guinness, Os. *Time For Truth*. Grand Rapids: Baker Books, 2000.

Hample, Zach. *How to Snag Major League Baseballs*. New York: Simon & Schuster, 2001.

Harbour, Brian. *Proclaim*, December 1980.

Hoezee, Scott. *Speaking As One*. Grand Rapids, MI: William B. Eerdmans, 1997.

Longenecker, Richard N. *Expositors Bible Commentary*, Volume 9. Grand Rapids, MI: Zondervan, 1981.

Lynch, Don *et al*. *Titanic: An Illustrated History*. New York: Hyperion, 1992.

MacDonald, Gordon. "Anatomy of a Spiritual Leader." *Leadership Journal*, Volume V, Number 4, Fall 1984.

McCullough, Donald W. *The Trivialization of God*. Colorado Springs: NavPress, 1995.

Mead, Frank S. *12,000 Religious Quotations*. Grand Rapids, MI: Baker Book House, 1989.

Myers, Kenneth A. *All God's Children and Blue Suede Shoes*. Wheaton, IL: Crossways Books, 1989.

Ortberg, John. *The Life You've Always Wanted*. Grand Rapids, MI: Zondervan, 1997.

Peck, M. Scott. *The Different Drum*. New York: Touchstone Books, 1998.

Peterson, Eugene H. *The Message*. Colorado Springs: NavPress, 2002.

—. *Under the Unpredictable Plant*. Grand Rapids, MI: William B. Eerdmans, 1992.

—. *Working the Angles*. Grand Rapids, MI: William B. Eerdmans, 1987.

Reilly, Rick. *Sports Illustrated*. March 20, 2000, back page.

Roberts, Vaughan. *Turning Points*. London: OM Publishing, 1999.

Schaller, Lyle. *Discontinuity and Hope*. Nashville: Abingdon, 1999.

Senge, Peter M. *The Fifth Discipline*. New York: Currency Doubleday, 1990.

"Shane." Paramount Pictures, 1952.

Shenk, Wilbert R. *Write the Vision*. Valley Forge, PA: Trinity Press International, 1995.

Sider, Ronald J. *Living Like Jesus*. Grand Rapids, MI: Baker Books, 1996.

Smedes, Lewis. *Shame and Grace*. HarperSanFrancisco, 1993.

Sproul, R.C. *The Soul's Quest For God*. Wheaton, IL: Tyndale House Publishers, 1992.

Starkey, Mike. *God, Sex, and the Search For Lost Wonder*. Downers Grove, IL: InterVarsity Press, 1997.

Willard, Dallas. *Hearing God*. Downers Grove, IL: InterVarsity Press, 1984.

—. *Renovation of the Heart*. Colorado Springs: NavPress, 2002.

—. *The Divine Conspiracy*. HarperSanFrancisco, 1998.

—. *The Spirit of the Disciplines*. HarperSanFrancisco, 1988.

Yancey, Philip. *Soul Survivor*. New York: Doubleday, 2001.

ANNOTATED RESOURCE GUIDE

Bailey, Kenneth E. *The Cross and the Prodigal.* St. Louis: Concordia Publishing House, 1973.
Drawing from a lifetime of personal experience amongst the villages of the Middle East, Bailey has written a classical exegesis of Jesus' most famous parable. This short book demonstrates why there has to be a party for the one who comes home to the Father.

Barna, George. *Growing True Disciples.* Ventura, CA: Issachar Resources, 2000.
Barna reveals, through research and conversations with pastors, that numerous congregations talk about discipleship but have no plan to bring it into the lives of their members.

Borthwick, Paul. *Six Dangerous Questions.* Downers Grove, IL: InterVarsity Press, 1996.
Although this book is primarily a call to involvement in world missions, Borthwick's half dozen paradigm-shifting questions serve as a wake-up call for anyone committed to church growth.

Bosch, David J. *Believing in the Future.* Valley Forge, PA: Trinity Press International, 1995.
This slim volume reveals the passion of one of the original launchers of the missional church movement. Bosch makes the case that American congregations need to re-disciple their own flocks in a post-modern culture.

Dodd, Brian J. *The Problem With Paul.* Downers Grove, IL: InterVarsity Press, 1996.
Dodd addresses the principle contemporary complaints about Christianity's most important early missionary: Was Paul neurotic, anti-Semitic, chauvinistic, and homophobic? Dodd helpfully steers readers into the context of Paul's first century world.

Foster, Richard. *Prayer.* HarperSanFrancisco, 1992.
The author of *Celebration of Discipline* here gathers reflections on 21 different modes of conversation with God. This book is unusually sensitive to the questions and fears of those just beginning to pray.

Frost, Michael, and Hirsch, Alan. *The Shaping of Things to Come.* Peabody, MA: Hendrickson Publishers, 2003.
Two Australian authors provide significant theological reflection and a wealth of practical guidance for the establishment of new emergent churches in post-Christian Western societies.

Kelly, Thomas. *A Testament of Devotion.* New York: HarperSan-Francisco, 1941.
For those leading a discipleship-oriented congregation, spiritual centering must be a way of life, not an optional or occasional exercise. This classic from the Quaker tradition is an enduring corrective to our present church culture's addiction to "muchness" and "manyness."

Myers, Kenneth A. *All God's Children and Blue Suede Shoes.* Wheaton, IL: Crossways Books, 1989.
Myers presents a compelling case that Western churches will inevitably fall short of their mission of releasing lifelong learners of Jesus unless their leaders confront Protestantism's unexamined embrace of popular culture.

Ortberg, John. *The Life You've Always Wanted.* Grand Rapids, MI: Baker Book House, 1997.
Ortberg manages to make the basic disciplines of Christian spirituality feel authentic and attainable for people trapped in the blur of contemporary Western life. Memorable examples and specific plans for forward progress abound.

Peterson, Eugene H. *Under the Unpredictable Plant.* Grand Rapids, MI: William B. Eerdmans, 1992.
It can be argued that every pastor ought to read this book every five years. From the wealth of his personal experience and reflection, especially on the matter of keeping the Sabbath, Peterson provides remarkably contemporary insights on pastoral leadership from the book of Jonah.

Rodin, R. Scott. *Stewards in the Kingdom: A Theology of Life in All Its Fullness.* InterVarsity Press, 2000.
Rodin wears the hat of a scholar who is providing a theological tour de force of the Church's use (and abuse) of the concept of stewardship. His book is dynamically practical, particularly as he dismantles the myth of the two kingdoms–that is, the assumption that disciples

have permission to jump back and forth between God's kingdom and a kingdom of their own making.

Schaller, Lyle. *Discontinuity and Hope.* Nashville: Abingdon, 1999. Should the dissolution of the "way we used to do things" on the American church scene create discouragement or optimism? Schaller, as always, opts for the latter, and provides compelling evidence that this is a God-provided kairos moment in Church history.

Shenk, Wilbert R. *Write the Vision.* Valley Forge, PA: Trinity Press International, 1995
This brief but insightful introduction to the concept of the missional church comes from one of the movement's original voices. Shenk reveals how the traditional Western notion of church membership has been superseded by the need for cutting edge discipleship.

Sider, Ronald J. *Living Like Jesus.* Grand Rapids, MI: Baker Books, 1996.
Known for pressing beyond typical church formulations for spirituality, Sider provides a wide-angle lens picture of what it means to imitate Christ.

Willard, Dallas. *The Divine Conspiracy.* HarperSanFrancisco, 1998. Richard Foster's foreword begins, "This is the book I have been searching for all my life." It is an extensive examination of Jesus' concept of the kingdom of God, especially as revealed in the Sermon on the Mount. As one who writes about the need to relentlessly pursue the way of Jesus, Willard has few equals.

_____ *Renovation of the Heart.* Colorado Springs: NavPress, 2002.
This contemporary classic concerning the New Testament's call to spiritual formation includes a closing chapter on congregational strategies for disciplemaking that is particularly helpful.

_____ *The Great Omission.* HarperSanFrancisco, 1998.
This valuable collection of articles and presentations, many of them previously unpublished, speaks to the challenges of calling the already-churched to full-bodied trust in Christ in a consumer-driven, postmodern environment.

Wink, Walter. *The Powers That Be*. New York: Doubleday, 1998.
A biblical scholar here brings together the salient points of his three monumental studies of the New Testament's concept of principalities and powers. It provides excellent case studies of how authentic discipleship must boldly follow the way of Jesus and not the tentative responses of formal Christianity.

Wright, N.T. *Simply Christian*. HarperSanFrancisco, 2006.
For those awaiting a worthy successor to C.S. Lewis' *Mere Christianity*, Wright provides a brief but effective synopsis of the essential case for Christianity. He moves effortlessly from the realms of philosophy and pre-evangelism to discipleship.

INDEX

ABOUT THE AUTHOR

Glenn McDonald is senior pastor of Zionsville Presbyterian Church in suburban Indianapolis, a congregation he helped organize in 1983, and which was named one of the *300 Excellent Protestant Congregations* in a study conducted by Paul Wilkes and funded by the Lilly Endowment (Westminster John Knox Press, 2001).

McDonald is also coauthor, with Ben C. Johnson, of *Imagining a Church in the Spirit* (Eerdmans, 1999) and a consultant on church growth for the Presbyterian Church USA. He holds a Master of Divinity Degree from Trinity Evangelical Divinity School, Deerfield, Illinois. He and his wife Mary Sue, both native Hoosiers, have four children: Mark, Katy, Jeff, and Tyler.